The
Restored
Life

in the Kingdom of God

Richard T. Case
& Lawrence A. Collett

**elevate
faith**

Published in Boise, Idaho by Elevate Faith, a division of Elevate Publishing. www.elevatepub.com

For information please email: info@elevatepub.com.

ISBN (print): 978-1937498733

Printed in the United States of America

TABLE OF CONTENTS

DEDICATION

We would like to dedicate this book to our families. They have demonstrated and lived "A Restored Life in the Kingdom," showing us the beauty and wonder of the Kingdom of God. There is no question God has enriched our lives and our journey through all of you. We treasure you and are committed to supporting and strengthening our families and their abiding relationships with Christ.

To our wives, Sherry Collett and Linda Case, we thank God for the oneness we have experienced and the joy of sharing our journey on earth together. What a gift you both are and we find love, joy, satisfaction, unity and fellowship in this unique, God-ordained and inspired relationship called marriage (50 years for the Colletts and 45 for the Cases). Thank you for your faith, love, commitment and willingness to pursue and join the work God has ordained for all four of us.

To our children, we are so thankful for your desire to grow and enrich your own family units and to remain supportive of our extended families. We count it a great blessing to have the honor of being your earthly fathers and to remain a part of your lives, continuing to participate in the growth, fellowship and maturation of your marriages and children as well. So thanks to Michele and Dave Maack, Mike and Paige Collett and Nicole and Chris Wilkerson; Peter and Shara Case, Michele Case and Christina and Mark Siebels. What great gifts you are!

Finally to our grandchildren, we are grateful and thankful for the blessing of being grandfathers and sharing time, events, insight and direction in so many ways. We see the Father equipping you for the future and instilling values and gifts that will reflect His image to others. The world you inherit and in which you dwell may provide obstacles for the growth, encouragement and strengthening of your faith. However, the God we serve is faithful and we are sure He will lead you to experience the fullness and joy of a restored life, regardless of the environment and circumstances you face. In so many ways we see the reality of the Kingdom in you and are excited by your joy, enthusiasm and energy. Our thanks to Joshua. Aidan, Nicole, Rachael, and Riley on the Case side and to Ellie, Christian, Annie, Morgan, Wes, Sam, Ally, Tad and Nat of the Collett clan. May your lives always reflect the optimism, peace and excitement of the Kingdom.

ACKNOWLEDGEMENTS

This book started as a suggestion by Larry to Rich. At the time, Rich and Linda were hosting a series of overseas couples' retreats. The retreats provided time for worship, Bible study (led by Rich), and sightseeing. After six or seven of these, and with the domestic seminars that were also held at their retreat center or other facilities, it was observed that a significant amount of the material presented was related and connected to a much bigger story. The suggestion was to begin to consolidate and combine this material into a single text that would illustrate and narrate this story.

At that same time, Rich and Linda were not only leading a ministry, but also assisting churches in an interim advisory or pastoral capacity. In addition, they were running a family business, which needed constant attention and direction. Thus, while acknowledging the need to proceed with such a project, the time was just not available to move forward. Therefore, Larry started assembling the material and began to develop a rough outline. Subsequently, Rich took the outline and put together an initial foundation of how the material should be connected and presented. At this time, it was predominantly a study guide. Later, the material was supplemented with more descriptive and explanatory commentary to expand the study into a book and reference text as well. Some of this was derived from Larry's unpublished study entitled "Kingdom Restoration."

Clearly, a book on restored living cannot be complete without reference to the collective experiences resulting from the existential reality of such a life. We have added incidents that describe true experiences of living a restored life. While some will discount these as isolated experiences, this could not be farther from the truth. A restored, Kingdom life produces supernatural activity with frequency. Some is invisible to the human eye, but very real and present to the heart. Other activity is not only visible, but beyond human explanation. When one abides with the Father, it is reasonable to see Him in action. There are many more incidents that could have been included in the book.

Our thanks to numerous parties for their assistance and support in getting this project completed. First, to our spouses for their generous allowance of the time needed to write, edit and publish the book. This project took over four years to complete. The number of hours spent in writing, compiling and reviewing were exhaustive. Sherry and Linda were both supportive and encouraging of this effort. We sincerely appreciate their perseverance and endurance through the period of development.

Also, we are deeply grateful to the many individuals and couples whose lives are a testimony to the veracity and applicability of the material in this book. This includes not only the various attendees of the seminars taught by Rich, but also those being mentored by both Rich and Larry through the CEO Forum. In addition, those individuals who continue to learn from their teaching provide a growing laboratory of real lives changed and enhanced by intentional movement to an abiding, Kingdom-driven relationship with the Father.

PREFACE

This book is the first of two books dealing with life: what one should expect from it and how it is to be lived. It is written from the perspective of a biblical life view. You will see scripture cited throughout. That is because the Bible is really about life: yours, ours, everyone's. It contains unique insight and knowledge of life's components, origin, purpose, destiny, expectations and results. It includes what we should desire and seek to experience and achieve.

Our objective is to move the reader from biblically based knowledge and theology to a vibrant, active relationship with the Father, through Jesus Christ. In that regard, this book is really about discipleship rather than evangelism. However, we recognize some readers may discover they never were aware the decision they made to accept Christ as Savior had such ramifications. Or perhaps they never really understood what they were accepting when they chose Christ. In any event, it is our desire to have the reader not only accept Jesus, but move forward to receive what He has provided.

Once we grasp that Jesus provided the opportunity for us to experience the life intended at creation, a whole new spectrum of living emerges. We are no longer "captured" by the actions of preceding generations or by the blunders we make on our own. We no longer need to ask, "What's life all about?" We no longer need to live life responding to the dynamic forces seeking to keep us from a restored life. Instead, we can diligently move forward as people with a mission and purpose. Our lives have focus. We understand where we are headed. We possess guidance, direction and counsel. Our relationships, work and activities have meaning and bear a distinct connection.

In this book, our goal is to articulate and define the reality of the life we can now experience because of the work of Christ, both during His time on Earth and in His continuing work in the heavenly and earthly realms. We are "new persons" as a result of Him and are able to once again receive the blessings and promises the Father has provided. This experience is available now. While a more robust dimension of that life will come, we can immediately begin to dive deeper and deeper into the reality of our eternal existence.

While there are different ways to approach this material, we have some guidelines that should be of assistance in gaining optimum value from your efforts. First, don't try to finish in a prescribed time period. Allow the Father to move you at His pace. Secondly, don't worry if you stay in one section longer than another. We purposely have not structured the material into specific time frames. It is best utilized when the reader allows daily time for study and reflection. Understanding the life Christ has provided and living this awesome, restored life in God's Kingdom is a daily activity. We often find ourselves "slipping" back into the world with its related systems and activities. Consistent exercise helps us retain a Kingdom focus and mindset.

Each chapter can refresh us and invigorate our journey into life in the Kingdom. Therefore, the study is also a reference guide to be used as we enter the various stages of a vibrant, active, abiding relationship with the Father.

Next, let the scriptures "speak". Don't over intellectualize their meaning. Allow time to discern what God is really saying. Read and ponder their meaning and application.

Also, it is important to recognize the adjustment to a fully restored life will probably take some time. Don't expect it to occur overnight. We've already had a lifetime of adapting to other lifestyles, activities, systems and measures. Detaching from them and shedding our "normal responses" usually can't happen right away.

Finally, our expectation is to witness and experience changed lives. Since we were made in our Father's image, we should expect the results of our lives to bear witness and resemble His reality. His nature and character should begin to emerge from our thoughts and actions. As that happens, we are expected to "pass it on" to succeeding generations and other relationships. Allow others to also experience the abundance of righteousness, peace and joy that has permeated our lives. May they grasp the reality of the love of God, the work of Jesus Christ and the joy and unity we all experience in Him.

INTRODUCTION

Let's get straight to the point! What is this life on Earth about and how is it to be lived? These are basic but critical questions that lead us to a variety of answers, conclusions and decisions. Unfortunately, we have a tendency to ignore the questions and instead allow our lives to be lived in response to the days and the times. The activities of the day, designed to allow us to eat, sleep, communicate, transport, entertain, educate and care for others, seem to absorb all our being. Time to contemplate the real purpose, strategy and direction of life goes untended.

The reality however, is that such a life is totally reactionary. It forces us to respond to political, economic, military, health and governmental forces in order to conform and adapt to the agenda of the day. We tend to measure "success" by our ability to do so and the ease or difficulty incurred in the process. Is this the standard God has provided?

One of the primary reasons for Jesus' tenure on Earth was to allow mankind to return to the "life" he was created to receive. Due to the Fall in the Garden of Eden, man was separated from the Father, with no access to the relationship God desired. Jesus ended that! Because of the work of Christ, the path to fellowship with the Father has been reopened. The life that had been created for us to live is again available. The "Kingdom of God" is not just a theological term or deferred objective, but a present and reachable reality. Our lives can interact with Kingdom resources and objectives and we can begin to experience all the Father had created for us. That is why it is called the "Restored Life." Jesus ended the separation and has ushered in the Kingdom. We can begin to receive the promises of God, **right now!**

So, how is this done? How does this reality impact the way we live and how do our lives reflect this access and relationship? What must we do to have the Kingdom begin to lead and direct us, initiating the course and direction of our lives? How does the reality of God's Kingdom both intersect and impact?

Experiencing the Kingdom is intended to be a normal part of our everyday life. Time not spent in the Kingdom is time spent in the world. It exposes us to opposing systems and forces. Living in the world means we miss the blessings of a Kingdom life. We live outside God's created intention and depend on the world's systems, structures and leaders to satisfy our needs. We lack peace and discover we are missing or deferring our eternity experience. At best, we live as carnal Christians, operating with self-will and determination versus walking with and setting our hearts and minds on the Spirit, God's will and His desires for our lives.

Therefore, to enjoy the abundant life promised by God, we are called to live full-time as Kingdom residents. We know our willingness and ability to dwell in the Kingdom tends to be difficult since we still have an earthly, sinful nature with "roots" in the world. Our desire should be to live as the "new man" (person), to sever those roots and be transformed into the nature of our Lord who gives us the power to live in the Kingdom.

This all happens as we live the restored life and experience the opposite reactions our worldly lives produce:

- we experience growth in trial

- we find joy in obedience

- we discover peace in Him

- we experience freedom in our daily walk with Him

- we live in "Him", with all the benefits of His abundant kingdom

We also discover all the promises provided in Christ are real, not just theological, intellectual or potentially available (positional). They happen in the Kingdom and thus in our life, while we walk here on Earth in the middle of enemy territory.

This study is prepared to assist the believer in reaching a whole new dimension of life, a Kingdom life, a life in the Spirit, the "abundant" life Christ has made available. It is our hope that all true followers of Jesus experience His presence in a bold, supernatural way, allowing them to recognize the reality of the Kingdom life, here and now. Let them "soar like eagles" above a worldly experience, to the heights and joys of a restored life spent in the Kingdom of God.

CHAPTER I

The Big Picture

What does a Kingdom life, lived in our present time on earth, entail? We all face many significant questions and issues on a daily basis. For example, why is the world in its present condition? How do I make decisions in light of worldly events? Do I really have an overall view of life and the world? How do I find peace in the midst of such stress and tension? Why is there so much pain?

Philosophers and theologians have debated these questions for thousands of years. A plethora of answers emerge, often with significant contrasts and opposing viewpoints. How does a Christian address such questions? The approach from a Kingdom-dwelling Christian is distinctive and unique. Here the basis for addressing issues in life and the answers to deep, foundational questions is one's relationship with God. The more personal, transparent and intimate that relationship, the greater the insight and wisdom available in our lives.

As we begin, we want to take inventory of some key questions to help us better understand the type of life we are living and where we stand in our relationship with the Father.

There are some indicators that reveal whether we are walking with God in His Kingdom, or walking as Christians, in the "self" and in the world's kingdom, in step with its systems and methods.

HOW IS MY WALK WITH GOD?

What is God saying to me?

So much of our lives are spent reacting to issues and events. We tend to base our reactions on our intellectual assessment of the situation, the circumstances surrounding the issue or how we feel in general about the occurrence. Often we pray for God's intervention in matters, expressing our thoughts, emotions and desires. But do we really know what God has to say? Are we just giving our best efforts and hoping it will work out well, or are we receiving real insight and direction from the Father?

If I am not sure what God is saying to me, do I believe I can hear from Him personally?

Clearly, if we do not believe God speaks to us today, it will be difficult for us to hear Him. Some Christians believe He does not. Unquestionably, numerous and significant tragedies have occurred because certain people claimed that "God told them," and in some cases the results were clearly contrary to what the Father wanted. Should we allow these events to totally separate us from receiving what He has to say, especially when Scripture says He is always speaking and desires a relationship with us? Or is there a lack of testimony about the reality of hearing from God, both from the pulpit as well as from other believers? Does the lack of support and modeling from others keep us from hearing God's voice? Is our relationship with the Father one of a religious structure, theological position or experiential reality that leaves this level of communication outside its boundaries?

Describe your personal time with God in the Word and in prayer. What level of intimacy are you experiencing?

What does my Bible study and prayer life really entail? For most of us, our study involves reading and attempting to grasp an understanding of what we see on the pages. We may even study the works of commentators and writers to clarify what has been written. Our time in prayer consists of telling God what is on our mind, our needs and requirements. In both areas we end up with satisfaction we have engaged God but not any clarification of what is happening, its impact on our lives or insight into the future.

What kind of "fruit" (results) is being produced in my life?

Is my life resulting in something observable, desirous or beneficial? Or is it achieving maintenance at best? Am I really having an impact for God and/or others? How significant is that impact? How would I know? Any business that does not produce positive results will not last for long. Eventually, it becomes unsustainable. Is that what is happening to our lives?

If not much fruit is being produced, what do I think is the reason?

Many people find excuses by comparing their environment with others. Because some people have access to more time, resources or opportunity, they may sense a benefit in doing things others are unable to accomplish. A look at many of the people God used in Scripture reveals an opposite principle. He can use anyone, anytime, anywhere to accomplish great things.

Others feel a sense of unworthiness. Why would God use a sinner like me to do His work? The problem with this position is we are all unworthy of the Father's blessings. That's why Christ was so instrumental in bringing us back to the Kingdom. Because of Jesus, we are again acceptable to God and able to be used by Him

Do I normally, frequently experience the supernatural work of God in my life?

What does the word "supernatural" really mean? It refers to that which transcends the order of the visible or observable universe or which is clearly attributable to God. How many times do we witness or experience such happenings? Do these events happen only rarely, if ever, in our lives? Or do we see such things often? Do we frequently have experiences that can only be a result of the Father's activity and recognize them as such?

If I do not experience much or any supernatural work in my life, do I believe it is possible, or no longer relevant for our days?

Some people believe supernatural activity in the world is over and occurred only for a period of time in earlier history. Others feel it can always be "explained" with more time to analyze or discover. Therefore, there really is nothing of a supernatural nature, only that which momentarily exceeds our knowledge or understanding. With such a belief, it would be difficult to recognize or experience anything of a true supernatural nature. Supernatural activity is the result of a supernatural relationship. Obviously, if we don't have such a relationship, it would be hard to recognize these types of occurrences. Or, if we have one but don't see, expect or anticipate a "God-sized" response, we probably aren't experiencing supernatural activity.

Do I understand and experience my ability to "loose and bind" in the spiritual realm?

Can we participate in supernatural activity or demonstrate and produce results, resources or activity that clearly is beyond our ability? Jesus says we can and points to Peter's proclamation that "you are the Christ, the son of the living God" (Matthew 16:16) as an example of such a revelation. Does God reveal wisdom, information or insight to us that allows us to act with such authority? Is this something we would like to frequently experience?

What are the main characteristics of my life? Is it full of fear, anxiety, worry, oppression, sadness and resignation, or of peace, joy and freedom?

Are we really satisfied with the life we are experiencing, or is there something missing that could make it full and complete? Are we constantly engaged in worldly trials and troubles creating continuous fear and dread? Do we expect life to be free of such events? How do we make this journey, confront such issues and have a sense of gratification and thanksgiving in the process? Is this possible?

INSIGHTS TO CONSIDER

"It is to be feared there are many earnest followers of Jesus from whom the meaning of this word (abiding), with the blessed experience it promises, is very much hidden. While trusting in their Savior for pardon and for help, and seeking to some extent to obey Him, they have hardly realized to what closeness of union, to what intimacy of fellowship, to what wondrous oneness of life and interest, He invited them when He said, 'Abide in Me.' This is not only an unspeakable loss to themselves, but the church and the world suffer in what they lose." (Andrew Murray, *Abide in Christ*)

In this statement, Andrew Murray illustrates the degree to which our Christian experience can fall short of all Christ enabled it to be. We have a tendency to settle for much less than Christ has made available. If we were given a choice of a free bicycle or Ford Explorer, I suspect we would choose the SUV. Yet, we usually choose to settle for the bicycle in our faith journey, even though we have been provided the ability to travel in the "royal carriage." Why do we do this? Part of the reason may be our lack of knowledge and insight into the fullness of Christ's provision.

There is a difference between living with God and living in relationship with God. One is existence; the other is life.

Being with God in our worldly walk still maintains focus on the world and our experience in that realm. God, at best, becomes a trusted confidant and advisor, but we ultimately make all the decisions and determine our course. We move from moment to moment on the basis of our knowledge and experience until time runs out. Living "in God" or "in Christ," brings the fullness of life. He is life and as we experience and seek more and more of Him, we enlarge the realm and nature of our life walk. We move beyond earthly living into the sphere of eternal life, now. It doesn't end at physical death. Our time here on Earth is the beginning of an eternal journey that constantly moves forward.

If one doesn't enter the "Promised Land," one's life is spent wandering.

When we grasp the completeness of Scripture, we understand that for us the Promised Land is really the Kingdom of God. However, like the Israelites, we must make the decision to enter in order to receive the promised blessings. These blessings are there, waiting for us to receive them, but we must enter and remain. Otherwise, we also will wander in this world, day by day, seeking what has already been provided. Life becomes a big "treasure hunt," where we look for clues and go to places seeming to offer the answers and benefits, only to come up empty at every door. We need to understand what the Promised Land really is, how we enter and what we must to do to stay in that realm.

SUMMARY

Based upon our answers to these questions, we may see a huge gap between our current relationship with God and the potential one He desires us to experience. These questions were designed to illustrate the magnitude of difference between the life Christ brought to reality and the life we may be living.

In Luke 4:43, Jesus states He was sent to this world to preach the "good news of the Kingdom of God." Obviously, this was central to His ministry. It is important we grasp this reality and the fact that Jesus was not talking about something we would find later (Matthew 4:17). He ushered it into reality now, and it is there to experience at this moment in history.

What thoughts do you have about the abundant life promised for those who dwell in the Kingdom daily? Also, what questions would you like this study to answer as you seek truth and practical steps to fully experience the Kingdom and a restored life?

_____

_____

_____

_____

_____

_____

_____

_____

_____

_____

A House Built Upon the Rock

Matthew 7:24-25

On August 24, 2008, the Sunday before the start of the Democratic National Convention in Denver, Colorado, our family experienced a miracle of God. It was a typical warm, sunny day in Colorado in August, with no forecast of bad weather. On this particular Sunday, our son, his wife, their two boys (ages 4 and 2) and our daughter were with us at home. We spent the afternoon in our theater watching *The Sound of Music*, our grandson's favorite movie. Around 5:15 PM, we all went outside on our east deck. We noticed a cloud above us with a long, thin white line hanging in it. We thought it was strange. Moreover, because there was no forecast of severe weather, and we have never experienced a tornado near the foothills of the Rocky Mountains, we thought it just a wind vortex that would pass. We had no concern until it dropped to the ground on the northwest corner of our house. We watched it grew darker as it vacuumed dirt from our property. We then knew it was a real tornado and was coming toward our house! As I realized the potential danger, I told everyone to go immediately into the basement to a safe room. I stayed outside and just watched. It still did not seem "real" and certainly it was not going to be a problem.

Then, it kicked into high gear, blasting the sound of a hundred locomotives I have heard others describe. It got darker and shrubs and trees were now flying by the house. I said to myself, *Oh, this is going to be bad; it's coming right toward our house. I'd better get inside, and now!* Being a believer in Christ and in the awesome power of our God, I asked the Father, "What are You going to do with this, and what do you want me to do?" He told me through the Holy Spirit, "Do not fear; I will protect you and your house as I have promised you in the covenant with My children. Stand against this evil that has come against you and your house and pray the covenant."

I had been studying and teaching others the wonderful promises of the covenant, which holds the fundamental understanding that God will bless me to become a blessing, with many provisions of safety, protection, deliverance and abundant life. So, I went to the glass doorway and stood there watching and praying as God had instructed. The tornado was coming directly toward our house, about one hundred yards away, and I just stood there and prayed for about six minutes. All of a sudden, it dissipated back up into the cloud, which was moving over the house. I thought, *Wow, that was amazing.* At least it's over and going to be moving away from the house. So, I went to the front glass door and looked out to watch the storm go away.

But it did not. In fact, the tornado re-formed right in front of our house and was now massive, over a quarter mile wide. It was not going away, but was coming back toward the house! It was at this point that a Channel 9 News helicopter, covering Democratic Convention arrivals, was in Castle Rock because the tornado had been spotted. It began taping the tornado around our house. Those first six minutes when it initially formed and came toward the house were not captured on film. I again just stood there and prayed the covenant, asking God to fulfill His promise of protecting our family and our house, even though it looked bleak. My wife Linda and my daughter Michelle had become concerned that I did not join them in the basement, so they came upstairs to look for me. They saw me praying with my hands pressed against the glass, so they came to the door, where they saw the massive tornado again coming directly at our house! They also sensed the Lord's protection and stood there with me, joining in prayer. Linda, was praying for the power of Christ to materialize. Michelle was praying for God to preserve the house, which is used for marriage retreats, asking Him to preserve this wonderful place where weak and broken marriages get restored and healed. Together, we stood together and prayed.

The tornado seemed to be going away and then it would just come back, back and forth right in front of our house, no more than a hundred yards away. At one point, the helicopter captured footage of the broad funnel cloud engulfing the house. The broadcasters from the live newscast, which had broken into the current Olympic coverage, commented that they thought the house was going to be destroyed. As the tornado pulled away, they could not believe the house was still there. We just kept praying. Then, after what seemed like hours, the funnel just disappeared back up into the cloud and was gone!! The video from the news shows eleven total minutes of this going back and forth at our house. It was truly a miraculous work of God that protected our family and retreat house. The remarkable video confirms the reality of this amazing story.

By the way, the sign of God's covenant is a rainbow. After the tornado was over, the sun came out and we looked out at a gigantic double rainbow! The God of the universe did an amazing work for us. His promise was real and He confirmed it for us through the rainbow. What was meant for evil and destruction was turned into good and wonder.

Channel 9 News sent a crew to our house for an interview, as they could not believe neither the house nor us were harmed. They rolled the camera as Linda told the story of the miracle, giving public testimony of the power of Christ and the miraculous, supernatural power of God that literally held back the force of the tornado and saved our family and our house. She explained the whole story and called it for what it was—a miracle. The station led its 9:00 PM and 10:00 PM news with her testimony and did not edit any of it, giving glory to God. They even finished the story with a statement that "it was a family of faith that saw God work on this amazing Sunday." *Wow!* The video shows what happened was indeed real; anyone, even those who do not believe in Christ or the supernatural, can sense it was a miracle due to a force not belonging to us. We give all the glory to God as we continue to rejoice we had the privilege of experiencing Him in this special way.

CHAPTER 2

The Necessity of Living a Restored Life in God's Kingdom

Despite being currently grounded on planet Earth, we still have the capacity to live in the Father's Kingdom. We may ask the question, "Why do I need to live such a life? Since I have already received my salvation, why do I need to move to a different realm of reality?"

To answer this, the Scriptures clearly point to the Kingdom. Colossians 1:13 states that the purpose of salvation is to direct us to such a life. Scripture is replete with references to the reality and effectiveness of Kingdom living. It is clear that living outside the Kingdom misses the fullness of the blessings we were created to receive and the life Christ restored through His work on earth.

To more fully grasp the elements of a Biblical life view leading us to this fully restored life, we need to understand the Bible from the perspective of a tapestry, where all its fabric is neatly woven together by the gentle, purposeful hands of its author. The main components of its pattern emerge.

CREATION

GENESIS 1:1-8, 26-31, AND 2:8-23

In the beginning God created the heavens and the earth. The earth was formless and void, and darkness was over the surface of the deep, and the Spirit of God was moving over the surface of the waters. Then God said, "Let there be light"; and there was light. God saw that the light was good; and God separated the light from the darkness. God called the light day, and the darkness He called night. And there was evening and there was morning, one day.

Then God said, "Let there be an expanse in the midst of the waters, and let it separate the waters from the waters." God made the expanse, and separated the waters, which were below the expanse from the waters which were above the expanse; and it was so. God called the expanse heaven. And there was evening and there was morning, a second day.

Then God said, "Let Us make man in Our image, according to Our likeness; and let them rule over the fish of the sea and over the birds of the sky and over the cattle and over all the earth, and over every creeping thing that creeps on the earth." God created man in His own image, in the image of God He created him; male and female He created them. God blessed them; and God said to them, "Be fruitful and multiply, and fill the earth, and subdue it; and rule over the fish of the sea and over the birds of the sky and over every living thing that moves on the earth." Then God said, "Behold, I have given you every plant yielding seed that is on the surface of all the earth, and every tree which has fruit yielding seed; it shall be food for you; and to every beast of the earth and to every bird of the sky and to every thing that moves on the earth which has life, I have given every green plant for food"; and it was so. God saw all that He had made, and behold, it was very good. And there was evening and there was morning, the sixth day.

14

The Lord God planted a garden toward the east, in Eden; and there He placed the man whom He had formed. Out of the ground the Lord God caused to grow every tree that is pleasing to the sight and good for food; the tree of life also in the midst of the garden, and the tree of the knowledge of good and evil.

Now a river flowed out of Eden to water the garden; and from there it divided and became four rivers. The name of the first is Pishon; it flows around the whole land of Havilah, where there is gold. The gold of that land is good; the bdellium and the onyx stone are there. The name of the second river is Gihon; it flows around the whole land of Cush. The name of the third river is Tigris; it flows east of Assyria. And the fourth river is the Euphrates. Then the Lord God took the man and put him into the Garden of Eden to cultivate it and keep it. The Lord God commanded the man, saying, "From any tree of the garden you may eat freely; but from the tree of the knowledge of good and evil you shall not eat, for in the day that you eat from it you will surely die." Then the Lord God said, "It is not good for the man to be alone; I will make him a helper suitable for him." Out of the ground the Lord God formed every beast of the field and every bird of the sky, and brought them to the man to see what he would call them; and whatever the man called a living creature, that was its name. The man gave names to all the cattle, and to the birds of the sky, and to every beast of the field, but for Adam there was not found a helper suitable for him. So the Lord God caused a deep sleep to fall upon the man, and he slept; then He took one of his ribs and closed up the flesh at that place. The Lord God fashioned into a woman the rib, which He had taken from the man, and brought her to the man. The man said, "This is now bone of my bones, and flesh of my flesh;

She shall be called Woman, because she was taken out of Man."

How did God's creation occur?

It happened by God speaking. The material was created by the spiritual; thus, all physical matter is subordinate and subject to the power and authority of God. The Earth was designed in an orderly and systematic way. God ascribed to it goodness at every step of the process.

Why did it occur?

The Genesis account shows the Creator providing the perfect environment for mankind. It was a place where all His intentions could be experienced.

What was the Creator's intent?

It was God's intent that we experience Him through fellowship and live the life He prepared for us. This life can be summarized in one word, **excellence**. God desired us to experience excellence in our relationship with Him, our spouses, our children and with each other. He wanted us to have excellent provision and to be successful in our work. He desired us to be morally pure and to have dominion over the rest of His creation. Finally, He wanted us to multiply in number and effectiveness.

The environment provided man at creation was very close, in reality, to the Kingdom of God. It was the place where we were to experience the fullness of life. It was designed for us to flourish.

THE FALL

GENESIS 3:1-13

> *Now the serpent was more crafty than any beast of the field which the Lord God had made. And he said to the woman, "Indeed, has God said, 'You shall not eat from any tree of the garden'?" The woman said to the serpent, "From the fruit of the trees of the garden we may eat; but from the fruit of the tree which is in the middle of the garden, God has said, 'You shall not eat from it or touch it, or you will die.'" The serpent said to the woman, "You surely will not die! For God knows that in the day you eat from it your eyes will be opened, and you will be like God, knowing good and evil." When the woman saw that*

the tree was good for food, and that it was a delight to the eyes, and that the tree was desirable to make one wise, she took from its fruit and ate; and she gave also to her husband with her, and he ate. Then the eyes of both of them were opened, and they knew that they were naked; and they sewed fig leaves together and made themselves loin coverings. They heard the sound of the Lord God walking in the garden in the cool of the day, and the man and his wife hid themselves from the presence of the Lord God among the trees of the garden. Then the Lord God called to the man, and said to him, "Where are you?" He said, "I heard the sound of You in the garden, and I was afraid because I was naked; so I hid myself." And He said, "Who told you that you were naked? Have you eaten from the tree of which I commanded you not to eat?" The man said, "The woman whom You gave to be with me, she gave me from the tree, and I ate." Then the Lord God said to the woman, "What is this you have done?" And the woman said, "The serpent deceived me, and I ate."

We see in this passage that from the beginning God allowed man the freedom to "opt out" of His creative intentions. He gave man free will to choose to receive His provision or to move to some other level of existence. He allowed the presence of alternatives so mankind could make such a choice. We know what happened. Man used his choice unwisely. He listened to ungodly counsel and chose not to follow the Creator's instructions.

The purpose of the test

The challenge was whether or not to accept God's provision and covenant (to obey or not). Man was given the choice. He still chooses! God does not force us into relationship but invites us into this intimacy through our choices, respecting our free will.

Mankind's failure

At the heart of man's disobedience was his failure to believe God. When confronted with a choice opposite of what God had spoken, man and woman did not go back to God to clarify His instruction to not eat of the "tree of the knowledge of good and evil". They thought the serpent's way was best and chose not to believe or understand the truth of God's instructions.

The eternal result

The consequences appeared in man's spiritual death (no longer in intimate fellowship with God, but driven by self-centeredness), his exile from Kingdom living in the Garden and his loss of innocence and fellowship with God. He was moved to a fallen world where the intentions of the Creator could no longer be naturally experienced. This is the current condition of our world. We are no longer in the perfect environment to experience the fullness and presence of His being. We are instead in enemy territory, constantly threatened by chaos, destruction and entropy. Our Kingdom presence and experience were removed, at least temporarily.

THE WORK OF CHRIST

COLOSSIANS 1:12-18

> *Giving thanks to the Father, who has qualified us to share in the inheritance of the saints in light. For He rescued us from the domain of darkness, and transferred us to the Kingdom of His beloved Son, in whom we have redemption, the forgiveness of sins. He is the image of the invisible God, the firstborn of all creation. For, by Him, all things were created, both in the heavens and on earth, visible and invisible, whether thrones or dominions or rulers or authorities—all things have been created through Him and for Him. He is before all things, and in Him all things hold together. He is also head of the body, the church; and He is the beginning, the firstborn from the dead, so that He Himself will come to have first place in everything.*

God had restoration in His plan for mankind from the beginning. He created man for eternity, not short-term pleasure. He had a much bigger picture in mind. Since the Fall, He has constantly been calling man to come back home. He clearly wants everyone re-aligned with His created intent. He has worked through patriarchs, prophets, judges, kings, rulers and disciples to pave the road for restoration. The door was finally opened through Jesus Christ. God physically entered the world through Christ and took residence within the hearts of men. He ensured relationship and restoration, unilaterally addressing a host of issues that had left man spiritually inept.

The need for the Father to send His son, Jesus Christ

In order to have a restored relationship, we needed to be covered with the holiness necessary to re-enter the presence of God. Man is unable to obtain this holiness by himself. Only Christ could provide the cover needed to return to the Father and His Kingdom.

What Christ did for us and for all mankind

There are so many facets to the work of Christ that it becomes difficult to define in its entirety. The chasm between man and God had become so great that a rebuilt relationship would require a massive undertaking. Christ accomplished this and in the process brought us peace, life, the ability to bear fruit, a new being, freedom and the riches of the Father's grace. In essence, He completely restored our relationship with the Father.

How did Christ accomplish this?

The simple answer is "He saved us". That salvation was all-encompassing and ensured our redemption, regeneration, repentance, adoption, purification, forgiveness, removal of condemnation, atonement, justification, reconciliation, sanctification and glorification. All these elements had to be addressed in order to get us back into a restored position with God. Indeed, how great a salvation we have been provided!

As a result of Christ's work, we are restored to our original position in Eden. This restoration is both immediate and progressive. We immediately have access upon the acceptance of Christ and His work. We progress to a more intimate restoration upon our physical, earthly death. The completeness and final stage of this restoration will occur later.

RE-CREATION

REVELATION 21:1 – 22:6

Then I saw a new heaven and a new earth; for the first heaven and the first earth passed away, and there is no longer any sea. And I saw the holy city, new Jerusalem, coming down out of heaven from God, made ready as a bride adorned for her husband. And I heard a loud voice from the throne, saying, "Behold, the tabernacle of God is among men, and He will dwell among them, and they shall be His people, and God Himself will be among them, and He will wipe away every tear from their eyes; and there will no longer be any death; there will no longer be any mourning, or crying, or pain; the first things have passed away."

And He who sits on the throne said, "Behold, I am making all things new." And He said, "Write, for these words are faithful and true." Then He said to me, "It is done. I am the Alpha and the Omega, the beginning and the end. I will give to the one who thirsts from the spring of the water of life without cost. He who overcomes will inherit these things, and I will be his God and he will be My son. But for the cowardly and unbelieving and abominable and murderers and immoral persons and sorcerers and idolaters and all liars, their part will be in the lake that burns with fire and brimstone, which is the second death."

Then one of the seven angels who had the seven bowls full of the seven last plagues came and spoke with me, saying, "Come here, I will show you the bride, the wife of the Lamb." And he carried me away in the Spirit to a great and high mountain, and showed me the holy city, Jerusalem, coming down out of heaven from God, having the glory of God. Her brilliance was like a very costly stone, as a stone of crystal-clear jasper. It had a great and high wall, with twelve gates, and at the gates twelve angels; and names were written on them, which are the names of the twelve tribes of the sons of Israel. There were three gates on the east and three gates on the north and three gates on the south and three gates on the west. And the wall of the city had twelve foundation stones, and on them were the twelve names of the twelve apostles of the Lamb.

The one who spoke with me had a gold measuring rod to measure the city, and its gates and its wall. The city is laid out as a square, and its length is as great as the width; and he measured the city with the rod, fifteen hundred miles; its length and width and height are equal. And he measured its wall, seventy-two yards, according to human measurements, which are also angelic measurements. The material of the wall was jasper; and the city was pure gold, like clear glass. The foundation stones of the city wall were adorned with every kind of precious stone. The first foundation stone was jasper; the second, sapphire; the third, chalcedony; the fourth, emerald; the fifth, sardonyx; the sixth, sardius; the seventh, chrysolite; the eighth, beryl; the ninth, topaz; the tenth, chrysoprase; the eleventh, jacinth; the twelfth, amethyst. And the twelve gates were twelve pearls; each one of the gates was a single pearl. And the street of the city was pure gold, like transparent glass.

I saw no temple in it, for the Lord God the Almighty and the Lamb are its temple. And the city has no need of the sun or of the moon to shine on it, for the glory of God has illumined it, and its lamp is the Lamb. The nations will walk by its light, and the kings of the earth will bring their glory into it. In the daytime (for there will be no night there) its gates will never be closed;

and they will bring the glory and the honor of the nations into it; and nothing unclean, and no one who practices abomination and lying, shall ever come into it, but only those whose names are written in the Lamb's book of life. Then he showed me a river of the water of life, clear as crystal, coming from the throne of God and of the Lamb, in the middle of its street. On either side of the river was the tree of life, bearing twelve kinds of fruit, yielding its fruit every month; and the leaves of the tree were for the healing of the nations. There will no longer be any curse; and the throne of God and of the Lamb will be in it, and His bondservants will serve Him. They will see His face, and His name will be on their foreheads. And there will no longer be any night; and they will not have need of the light of a lamp nor the light of the sun, because the Lord God will illumine them; and they will reign forever and ever. And he said to me, "These words are faithful and true"; and the Lord, the God of the spirits of the prophets, sent His angel to show to His bondservants the things which must soon take place.

In God's "big picture," life on Earth will not remain as it is. There will be spiritual and physical restoration, and heaven and earth will be re-made. We, too, will be completely unified once more. While the final product will look much like Eden, it will be a new creation.

The necessity of re-creation

As a result of the Fall, not only had man's spiritual condition changed, but so did his physical state, and the nature of his surroundings. Everything was exceedingly imperfect. Disasters of all kind had become so commonplace they were referred to as natural. Clearly, they were anything but natural, and God's eternal plan does not tolerate such an environment. His re-creation will put all things back in their original, intended form.

The means of re-creation

While the details are sometimes sketchy or difficult to understand, it is apparent that God will undertake this re-creation in a series of events, some which appear to be violent and cataclysmic. Those already residing in the Kingdom will be spared some of this calamity, but all will witness the "re-engineering" of the universe to conform to God's specifications. The highlight will be the physical restoration of our bodies in complete unity and presence with the Father. Once again, we will physically and spiritually dwell with Him in His Kingdom.

KINGDOM PARTICIPATION

REVELATION 3:20-22

Behold, I stand at the door and knock; if anyone hears My voice and opens the door, I will come in to him and will dine with him, and he with Me. He who overcomes, I will grant to him to sit down with Me on My throne, as I also overcame and sat down with My Father on His throne. He who has an ear, let him hear what the Spirit says to the churches.

REVELATION 22:17

The Spirit and the bride say, "Come." And let the one who hears say, "Come." And let the one who is thirsty come; let the one who wishes take the water of life without cost.

The purpose of God's plan as outlined in this chapter is to allow us to re-enter the fullness of God's domain, His presence and His being. This was His desire in the first place. He never gave up and continued to pursue and invite us back home. Through Christ, this has happened. Now we again have full access to the Father and His Kingdom.

So what does this Kingdom look like? How do our lives differ when we dwell there? How do our earthly lives interact? How do we get in?

The Appearance

We need to remember the Kingdom of God is not of this world. Therefore, if we are looking for a tangible representation in a worldly environment, we will not find it. The Kingdom is visible only to spiritually sensitive eyes. Its visibility is an extension of its activity. Its reality is embodied in its experiential truth and validity. In other words, we need to be there in order to know it is there.

The Entrance?

One can gain access to the Kingdom only through the life-giving, saving work of Jesus Christ. Any personal or individual quest of this "Holy Grail" will be fruitless. Jesus is the only way in. When we place our lives and trust in Him and accept all He did on our behalf, He provides us the opportunity to enter. He is the only way. Any life not placed in the person and deity of Jesus Christ will remain outside the Kingdom.

An exciting thing happens when we accept Jesus and place our lives in His hands. We receive the "indwelling of the Trinity." This is a theological expression of saying the Father, Son and Holy Spirit all take residence within us. This mystical union forms the basis of our Kingdom experience.

Its Characteristics

When we pursue the Kingdom with a passion that exceeds our desire for anything else in our lives, we are empowered with wisdom, resources and experiences unavailable elsewhere. Our lives may appear unconventional in a worldly sense, because they are lived in alignment with a King whose ways and activities often run counter to the systems and methods of the earth and its rulers.

One of the characteristics we can expect to see is a sense of transparent humility driven by a better understanding of the awesomeness of the King. We desire to have our lives changed to conform to His standards and in obedience to what He asks us to do. Our sin becomes intolerable as we rush to confess and allow Him to change us to conform to His image. We also seek to be of service to Him and can expect assignments that will take us wherever He desires, often to those with deep needs or requiring assistance in meeting some of life's basic requirements.

We can expect to face challenges, usually daily, in order to remain an effective and active Kingdom dweller. Jumping back into the world with its own goals and objectives is one of our biggest challenges. So also will be our continuing desire to let "self" rule our agenda and activities. We learn that endurance and perseverance are critical personality characteristics that typify a Kingdom dweller. Because we are still rooted on earth, we will still experience failure. But we remain focused on what lies ahead and realize this is an eternal journey. We move back into our Kingdom experience, not dwelling on the past.

Its Impact

When we reside in the Kingdom, we have access to all the King possesses. Therefore, we should expect to see His power effected in our lives. We watch supernatural results occur and see spectacular growth. We experience His rule and authority impacting others. We share in His peace and joy, because we are in His presence. The greatest experience of being in the Kingdom is just being with the King. There, we sense the fullness of His being and grasp that our lives are being lived to the greatest extent. In response to this, we develop a deep desire to see the Kingdom advance on Earth. We move beyond the boundaries of earthly logic in making decisions and undertaking activities. We transfer our thoughts, actions, and communion with the Father into His realm, not ours. We derive our existence from the love and power of the Father, with whom we become aligned and obedient.

Staying in the Kingdom

While we have gained access to the Kingdom through Christ, we still must choose to enter. And, when we leave we must choose to re-enter. Staying in the Kingdom requires daily surrender to the Father and turning over our schedules and agendas to His direction. The key is to develop an "abiding relationship" in which we consistently communicate with the Father, hear and understand His wishes and obediently adhere to His will.

If we desire to see our lives aligned with their original design and if we wish to experience all that God has in store for us, we will actively pursue the restored, Kingdom life. It is unfathomable to think we would desire anything else. But, unfortunately, we often settle for less than the abundant, excellent life God has provided. Let us put aside all else and enter with thanksgiving the Kingdom God has prepared!

SUMMARY

The whole of Scripture relates to the entrance and advancement of God's Kingdom. It was central to the work of Christ during His time on earth. The Kingdom is where creation and re-creation are focused, because it is the only location for "real" life to be experienced, now and eternally.

We have a choice every day: Are we going to live in this wonderful Kingdom or stay in the flesh, the self or the world's kingdom? The Father's heart and invitation is for us to choose His Kingdom restored life, so our lives bear witness to its reality. He wants us to join His bigger story, which is advancing the Kingdom and transferring more of mankind from the world to His Kingdom.

The disciples considered Jesus and His message so important they gave Him first priority in order to walk with Him (Mark 1:16-20). By doing so, they were starting to experience the Kingdom Jesus was bringing to reality on Earth. His charge to them was to take the message and experience of the Kingdom to all people everywhere and allow them the opportunity to receive its impact (Matthew 28:16-20; Acts 1:6-8). The result was changed lives, both for the disciples and those impacted by their Kingdom activity (Luke 9:1-6; 10:1-20). Today, He still calls us to do the same. Stay with Him, by definition in His Kingdom, and watch its supernatural resources and power bring life to our earthly walk. Experiencing the Kingdom is the thread of God's eternal tapestry. We can be part of His unbelievable generosity or opt out. Why would we want to do this? Sounds ridiculous, but we do so every time we choose to avoid an abiding relationship with Christ. In essence, we are saying our plan is better. Why would we make such a choice? We probably are unaware of the eternal consequences. Let us choose from this point forward to join the Father in His work and leave our own agenda behind.

Have you ever studied the Bible from the perspective of a life and world view? Most of us knew it was embedded within the whole of scripture, but never saw it described this way. It is exciting to recognize the Bible provides the framework for our lives and we can trust its design and content. If we accept its foundations for life, what impact would that have on the way we are currently living? How would it affect the way we schedule and plan our time? What would it change about the direction and pace we are experiencing? In the space below, write your answers to these questions and any other insights regarding life and the Kingdom of God.

_____

_____

_____

_____

_____

_____

An Example of Restoration

During one of our retreats, a couple came in the door. We could see and discern they were under heavy burden and oppression. They participated like everyone else, but did not share any of their heaviness. The last exercise of our retreat involves spending time alone, hearing from God. When they returned to share, God's word to them was to let go of their burden and receive His plan for restoration, which they were excited to pursue. They left with that heaviness lifted and understood that developing a intimate, abiding relationship with God was critical to receiving the promises.

The next day, I received a call from the husband, wanting to have lunch. When we met, he began to share the details of a deep financial hole he had dug for his family. After each statement, I would remark that God could still restore this, and he would respond, "Well, that is not all." He then would go on to describe the next complication that had further deepened the hole. This happened five times in a row. He was in serious trouble and because of all the complications, it appeared restoration would never be possible.

I asked him if he believed the promises he and his wife received at the retreat. He said it was uplifting to know that God speaks His promises, but it seemed overwhelming to trust they could become reality. I stated that God is faithful, nothing is too difficult for Him and He gives faith to possess the promises. They are always potential and not guaranteed, as His promises are delivered in His Kingdom, where we have a intimate, abiding relationship with Him. The condition to receiving the promises of a restored life is to abide and walk with Him. I asked this husband if he was willing to learn to abide and experience God's restoration of this most awful situation. He said yes, and his wife joined him.

Their testimony is now truly amazing, as God has brought restoration to them from the depths of the pit, and they are beginning to experience the promised abundant life. This is the beauty of the Gospel! It matters not where we start. God invites us to experience His full restoration to the grand life He desires to give. It is a beautiful thing to behold as we witness firsthand this restoration process.

CHAPTER 3

The Basis of an Intimate Relationship with the Father

As we begin pursuing a fully restored Kingdom life, we will face difficulty in staying on course and constantly engaging the Father. The chart at the end of this chapter was designed to provide a big picture of "Kingdom reality." The need to recognize and accept this reality is important in experiencing the restored life.

The Kingdom of God is another sphere of reality. As we see in John 18:33-37, it is not part of the world in which we physically reside; however, Matthew 6:10 shows that it still can impact this world. In Luke 17:20-21, we find that for us, at this time, it is an internal, spiritual dimension that is not physically observable, but nonetheless real. Scripture exhorts our lives to bear witness to the Kingdom. Our pursuit of Christ and His Kingdom leads to a relationship where we begin to hear His voice. In the Kingdom, there is a passion for truth. We further discover that the power generated in the Kingdom is from God. We are told in Matthew 6:10 that Kingdom life means allowing God to work through us. We find the Kingdom is the foundation of our confession, and there we take hold of eternal life (1 Timothy 6:12-14).

A key component of repentance is turning our lives to the Kingdom (Mark 1:14-15). Therefore, a constant awareness and acceptance of Kingdom reality and significance is necessary for restored life to begin. The restored life is a Kingdom life.

It becomes critical to intentionally commit to dwell in God's Kingdom and allow His resources to impact all areas of our lives (Ephesians 2:6-7; Colossians 3:1-3). As indicated in the chart, the only way this happens is through an abiding relationship with Christ. Christ is our "passage" (way) to this experience and only through Him can it be received.

As we seek Christ and the Kingdom, we encounter all kinds of obstacles trying to get in our way and throw us off track. This is clarified in the "Parable of the Sower." Furthermore, it is important for us to understand the essential components of an abiding relationship. In this chapter, we will analyze both topics, which will give us a better understanding of the need for focus and relationship with the Father.

"PARABLE OF THE SOWER"

MATTHEW 13:3-23

And He spoke many things to them in parables, saying, "Behold, the sower went out to sow; and as he sowed, some seeds fell beside the road, and the birds came and ate them up. Others fell on the rocky places, where they did not have much soil; and immediately they sprang up, because they had no depth of soil. But when the sun had risen, they were scorched; and because they had no root, they withered away. Others fell among the thorns, and the thorns came up and choked them out. And others fell on the good soil and *yielded a crop, some a hundredfold, some sixty, and some thirty. He who has ears, let him hear." And the disciples came and said to Him, "Why do You speak to them in parables?" Jesus answered them, "To you it has been granted to know the mysteries of the kingdom of heaven, but to them it has not been granted. For whoever has, to him more shall be given, and he will have an abundance; but whoever does *not have, even what he has shall be taken away from him. Therefore I speak to them in parables; because while seeing they do not see, and while hearing they do not hear, nor do they understand. In their case the prophecy of Isaiah is being fulfilled, which says, 'You will keep on hearing, but will not understand; You will keep on seeing, but will not perceive;*

> *For the heart of this people has become dull,*
> *With their ears they scarcely hear,*
> *And they have closed their eyes,*
> *Otherwise they would see with their eyes,*
> *Hear with their ears,*
> *And understand with their heart and return,*
> *And I would heal them.'*

But blessed are your eyes, because they see; and your ears, because they hear. For truly I say to you that many prophets and righteous men desired to see what you see, and did not see it, and to hear what you hear, and did not hear it.

"Hear then the parable of the sower. When anyone hears the word of the kingdom and does not understand it, the evil one comes and snatches away what has been sown in his heart. This is the one on whom seed was sown beside the road. The one on whom seed was sown on the rocky places, this is the man who hears the word and immediately receives it with joy; yet he has no firm root in himself, but is only temporary, and when affliction or persecution arises because of the word, immediately he falls away. And the one on whom seed was sown among the thorns, this is the man who hears the word, and the worry of the world and the deceitfulness of wealth choke the word, and it becomes unfruitful. And the one on whom seed was sown on the good soil, this is the man who hears the word and understands it; who indeed bears fruit and brings forth, some a hundredfold, some sixty, and some thirty."

Different places the seed can dwell

From this parable, we see many places where seed can fall. One is the path, a well-traveled place where the soil is well compacted and hard due to constant use. It is difficult for new seed to grow in such a place. Another is rocky soil, where there is a lack of depth and root systems due to the base underneath. And where there is a lot of brush and wild growth present, it is also difficult for seed to germinate. There just isn't enough soil available. Finally, we learn there is good soil that awaits the seed and provides a good environment for further activity.

What happens to the seed in each position?

Seed that has fallen on a path will generally remain on top of the path and will be carried away by other parties. In the parable, that other party is the Evil One, who will make sure it doesn't travel deeper into the soil. Seed in rocky soil may start to grow, but cannot withstand the heat and weather and eventually withers due to the lack of nutrients and depth. Likewise, seed sown among other growth becomes overwhelmed by the other plants and fails to properly grow and mature. But seed in good soil develops a strong root system and grows into a productive plant.

The reason for such a result

Christ equates the seed that falls on the path to a believer's lack of understanding. This understanding has no depth and the seed cannot develop to any extent. It remains in the soil but for a short time.

Seed in rocky soil is comparable to a person whose convictions and principles fall apart during adverse times or circumstances. They simply have not become established enough to persevere and endure such events.

The "worries of life and deceitfulness of wealth" overwhelm those who are crowded with other activities and priorities. They consume time and detract focus needed to allow the Kingdom to penetrate their lives.

Finally, we see that good soil is characterized by a life that is open to hearing and understanding what God has to say. Essentially, the Kingdom and the King become the focus of such a life.

The parable clearly points to a life that is sown and grown in the Kingdom and able to withstand obstacles the world is constantly throwing our way.

How should we respond?

A. Pursue wisdom

JAMES 1:5-8

> *But if any of you lacks wisdom, let him ask of God, who gives to all generously and without reproach, and it will be given to him. But he must ask in faith without any doubting, for the one who doubts is like the surf of the sea, driven and tossed by the wind. For that man ought not to expect that he will receive anything from the Lord, being a double-minded man, unstable in all his ways.*

"In Him you are, and in Him the wisdom is; dwelling in Him, you dwell in the very fountain of all light; abiding in Him, you have Christ the wisdom of God leading your whole spiritual life, and ready to communicate, in the form of knowledge, just as needful for you to know." (Andrew Murray, *Abide in Christ*)

The key to hearing and receiving wisdom from God is to believe He will speak to us and give us His revelation of wisdom about the questions we are asking. While we may struggle with what He says at first (this may take further processing and clarification), we recognize when we ask Him for answers, He will freely provide them.

B. Expect to hear His voice

JOHN 10:1-5, 27-30

> *Truly, truly, I say to you, he who does not enter by the door into the fold of the sheep, but climbs up some other way, he is a thief and a robber. But he who enters by the door is a shepherd of the sheep. To him the doorkeeper opens, and the sheep hear his voice, and he calls his own sheep by name and leads them out. When he puts forth all his own, he goes ahead of them, and the sheep follow him because they know his voice. A stranger they simply will not follow, but will flee from him, because they do not know the voice of strangers...*

> *...My sheep hear My voice, and I know them, and they follow Me; and I give eternal life to them, and they will never perish; and no one will snatch them out of My hand. My Father, who has given them to Me, is greater than all; and no one is able to snatch them out of the Father's hand. I and the Father are one.*

We are His sheep. We are to know Him, hear Him speak, and willingly follow Him. We need to listen to, have affection for, and follow Jesus.

THE ESSENCE OF ABIDING

The following Scriptures from the Word of God describe what constitutes an abiding relationship.

1. JOHN 15:1-5

> *I am the true vine, and My Father is the vinedresser. Every branch in Me that does not bear fruit He takes away; and every branch that bears fruit He prunes, that it may bear more fruit. You are already clean because of the word which I have spoken to you. Abide in Me, and I in you. As the branch cannot bear fruit of itself, unless it abides in the vine, neither can you, unless you abide in Me. I am the vine, you are the branches. He who abides in Me, and I in him, bears much fruit; for without Me you can do nothing.*

When one looks at this passage, we see the key to abiding is to stay connected to Christ. Note that Christ clearly states, "Apart from Me you can do nothing." Abiding is critical to living out this intimate life and enjoying the fruit of life He creates. We must stay in communication and fellowship with Christ in order to abide with Him.

2. John 17:21-26

...That they may all be one; even as You, Father, are in Me and I in You, that they also may be in Us, so that the world may believe that You sent Me. The glory which You have given Me I have given to them, that they may be one, just as We are one, I in them and You in Me, that they may be perfected in unity, so that the world may know that You sent Me, and loved them, even as You have loved Me. Father, I desire that they also, whom You have given Me, be with Me where I am, so that they may see My glory which You have given Me, for You loved Me before the foundation of the world. O righteous Father, although the world has not known You, yet I have known You; and these have known that You sent Me; and I have made Your name known to them, and will make it known, so that the love with which You loved Me may be in them, and I in them.

Abiding consists of a closeness that brings us unity with the Father. This unity will clearly reflect the Father. Abiding produces intimacy of fellowship with the Father and with Christ. It allows us to experience the love that is only found in His presence.

3. John 15:7-9

If you abide in Me, and My words abide in you, ask whatever you wish, and it will be done for you. My Father is glorified by this, that you bear much fruit, and so prove to be My disciples. Just as the Father has loved Me, I have also loved you; abide in My love.

Abiding produces results in our lives that are ordered, directed and accomplished through the Father. We experience the benefits of being a follower of Christ. We can expect abiding to impact our prayer lives and our circumstances.

SUMMARY

The abiding process is where God's wisdom, knowledge, guidance, direction and resources are transferred to man. Therefore, for us to acknowledge, receive and utilize the inheritance provided by the Father, we must be in this relationship. Otherwise, we are always limited to our own resources or those of the world, all which are limited and incomparable to those of the Kingdom.

In order to abide, we must make time for the Father. This goes beyond prayer and Bible study, though they are a part of the process. It means we just spend time in communication with Him.

We must not reduce our "abiding" experience to an assigned task or activity. Otherwise it becomes ritualistic and ordinary. This is a time for us to come into the presence of the Father, commune with Him and allow Him to reveal all He wants us to hear. It is our moment with the Creator and Sustainer of the universe, the Author and Provider of meaning and purpose in Life. In fact, He *is* life!

Therefore, we should develop a passion for time with the Father. It should become our highest desire to just be with Him. If we think of the closest relationship we have, we understand the need for it to cultivated and nurtured. Our feelings for the Father should supersede even our most precious earthly relationships.

Questions to consider:

a. **What are your thoughts regarding what a hearing and understanding heart feels and looks like?**

b. **Where are you in regard to your heart condition and reception to the Word of God? Are you spending sufficient time just having a conversation with God?**

c. **Write down your thoughts regarding your current position in the abiding process. How might you be challenged to adjust your life to learn how to abide and have intimacy with the Father? What questions do you have about the abiding process?**

_____

_____

_____

_____

_____

_____

_____

_____

_____

_____

_____

_____

_____

_____

_____

LIVING THE RESTORED LIFE:

CHAPTER 4

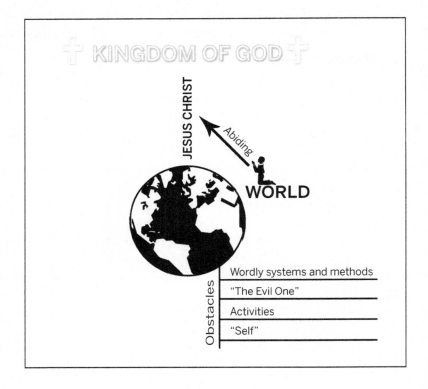

What Is a
"Restored Life"?

In previous chapters, we looked at the reality of the Kingdom of God and the need for us to have a constant focus and abiding relationship with the Father. We looked at a Biblical view of life from creation through eternity in the Kingdom. We discovered for our lives to be properly aligned with the Father's plan, we must be Kingdom dwellers.

In this chapter, we will explore in detail what really constitutes Kingdom life, what it brings to reality and what we can expect to experience. While all the chapters in this book flow together and are interrelated, this one is fundamental to defining, engaging and understanding the restored life. When we finish, we need to ask ourselves whether we want to take hold of the life prepared for us and whether we are committed to living in a manner that allows it to happen.

DESCRIPTION

The restored life Jesus promises has certain qualities intended to truly transform and give us His power to live and stay in the Kingdom.

1. A life that is "reborn" (regenerated)

JOHN 3:3-5

> Jesus answered and said to him, "Truly, truly, I say to you, unless one is born again he cannot see the kingdom of God." Nicodemus said to Him, "How can a man be born when he is old? He cannot enter a second time into his mother's womb and be born, can he?" Jesus answered, "Truly, truly, I say to you, unless one is born of water and the Spirit he cannot enter into the kingdom of God."

2 CORINTHIANS 5:17

> Therefore if anyone is in Christ, he is a new creature; the old things passed away; behold, new things have come.

TITUS 3:5

> He saved us, not on the basis of deeds, which we have done in righteousness, but according to His mercy, by the washing of regeneration and renewing by the Holy Spirit.

Why is this necessary?

Being reborn is necessary for restoration to the original life and Kingdom provided by God. When Adam and Eve sinned, the life of the Spirit in them ceased. All their offspring, including us, have a sin nature, which is comprised of flesh (material) and soul (the seat of the will, emotions, intellect and personality). This sin nature is naturally self-centered and operates upon one's will and agenda. Thus, in order to enter the Kingdom of God, it is necessary that the Spirit-filled life be restored within our nature. When that occurs, we again have the original three parts to our existence (flesh, soul, and spirit). This gives us the capacity to reestablish a relationship with God Almighty, which can only happen spirit to Spirit (when our spirit can again communicate with His). Rebirth happens when we receive Christ into our life. He makes us a new creature by placing his Spirit (the Holy Spirit) in us.

It is important to recognize this is a natural result of our decision to accept Christ, whether we are aware of it or not. We are new people. Christ has made this happen. We need not doubt it has occurred. Our response is to begin to live with that new spirit, not to worry about whether it has happened. Our faith in Christ and what He has done will lead to our experience of the reality of being reborn when we step out in faith and begin to live the new relationship our spirit has with the Father.

2. A life that is "transformed"

EZEKIEL 11:19

And I will give them one heart, and put a new spirit within them. And I will take the heart of stone out of their flesh and give them a heart of flesh.

ROMANS 12:1-2

Therefore I urge you, brethren, by the mercies of God, to present your bodies a living and holy sacrifice, acceptable to God, which is your spiritual service of worship. And do not be conformed to this world, but be transformed by the renewing of your mind, so that you may prove what the will of God is, that which is good and acceptable and perfect.

2 CORINTHIANS 3:16-18

...But whenever a person turns to the Lord, the veil is taken away. Now the Lord is the Spirit, and where the Spirit of the Lord is, there is liberty. But we all, with unveiled face, beholding as in a mirror the glory of the Lord, are being transformed into the same image from glory to glory, just as from the Lord, the Spirit.

How does this happen?

As we live in the Kingdom of God, we will be transformed from our old nature (sin nature) into our new nature. It is His work and not ours. He is the one who has put His Spirit within us to take us step by step into transformation (metamorphosis). This does not occur all at once, but is a lifetime of changing our nature, according to His will and His unique path for us, so we will experience more and more freedom. This happens during the journey, not only when it is finished. We are able to hear and understand the will of God as He leads us by His Spirit into His Kingdom.

3. A life that is renewed

ROMANS 12:2

> *And do not be conformed to this world, but be transformed by the renewing of your mind, so that you may prove what the will of God is, that which is good and acceptable and perfect.*

EPHESIANS 4:24

> *...And put on the new self, which in the likeness of God has been created in righteousness and holiness of the truth.*

2 CORINTHIANS 4:16

> *Therefore we do not lose heart, but though our outer man is decaying, yet our inner man is being renewed day by day.*

COLOSSIANS 3:9-10

> *Do not lie to one another, since you laid aside the old self with its evil practices, and have put on the new self who is being renewed to a true knowledge according to the image of the One who created him.*

What occurs as we are renewed?

Renewal means our old nature (sin nature) is being replaced with the new nature, that is Christ's nature. We are restored back to the original likeness of God, in whose image we were created. This restores us to righteousness, holiness, truth and experiencing the true image of God. Remember, after the Fall, we lost the ability to live the life God intended us to have at Creation. We defaulted to a worldly nature. Thankfully, Christ has renewed our being so it is capable of receiving true life again. When something is renewed or restored, it assumes its original condition. Such is the case for our new life in Christ.

4. A life that is united with the Trinity

EPHESIANS 2:5-6

> *Even when we were dead in our transgressions, [God] made us alive together with Christ (by grace you have been saved), and raised us up with Him, and seated us with Him in the heavenly places in Christ Jesus…*

JOHN 14:23-26

> *Jesus answered and said to him, "If anyone loves Me, he will keep My word; and My Father will love him, and We will come to him and make Our abode with him. He who does not love Me does not keep My words; and the word which you hear is not Mine, but the Father's who sent Me. These things I have spoken to you while abiding with you. But the Helper, the Holy Spirit, whom the Father will send in My name, He will teach you all things, and bring to your remembrance all that I said to you."*

In what way are we united?

In order for us to be truly transformed, we actually cannot operate on our own, performing in ways we believe will please God. Rather, the Trinity must be resident (dwelling) within so He can complete the work of transformation in us. Without the Trinity abiding in us, there will be no transformation. Again, what a blessing that Christ caused this to happen! As a result of His work on the cross and through faith in Him, we have the Trinity residing within us. This unity has been re-established. So has the promise of Ezekiel 36:26-27 been fulfilled: "And I will give you a new heart, and a new spirit I will put within you. And I will remove the heart of stone from your flesh and give you a heart of flesh. And I will put my Spirit within you and cause you to walk in My statutes and be careful to obey My rules."

5. A life that experiences God's original, created intent to live exceptionally and abundantly as a child of the King

ISAIAH 61:1-4

The Spirit of the Lord GOD is upon me, because the LORD has anointed me to bring good news to the afflicted; He has sent me to bind up the brokenhearted, to proclaim liberty to captives and freedom to prisoners; to proclaim the favorable year of the LORD and the day of vengeance of our God; to comfort all who mourn, to grant those who mourn in Zion, giving them a garland instead of ashes, the oil of gladness instead of mourning, the mantle of praise instead of a spirit of fainting. So they will be called oaks of righteousness, the planting of the LORD, that He may be glorified. Then they will rebuild the ancient ruins, they will raise up the former devastations; and they will repair the ruined cities, the desolations of many generations.

LUKE 4:14-21

And Jesus returned to Galilee in the power of the Spirit, and news about Him spread through all through the surrounding district. And He began teaching in their synagogues and was praised by all. And He came to Nazareth, where He had been brought up; and as was His custom, He entered the synagogue on the Sabbath, and stood up to read. And the book of the prophet Isaiah was handed to Him. And He opened the book and found the place where it was written, "The Spirit of the Lord is upon me, because He anointed me to preach the Gospel to the poor. He has sent me to proclaim release to the captives, and recovery of sight to the blind, to set free those who are oppressed, to proclaim the favorable year of the Lord." And He closed the book, gave it back to the attendant and sat down; and the eyes of all in the synagogue were fixed on Him. And He began to say to them, "Today this Scripture has been fulfilled in your hearing."

JOHN 10:10

The thief comes only to steal and kill and destroy; I came that they may have life, and have it abundantly.

What are some of the elements of this life?

Christ's first statement of ministry occurred at a synagogue in his hometown of Nazareth. He repeated Isaiah 6:1-4, stating this was fulfilled in Him. His purpose in coming was not just to give us a ticket to Heaven; rather, it was to restore the "life" of the Garden of Eden back into our lives here on Earth. The qualities of this life include:

- Healing

- Freedom

- Release from bondage and wounds

- Release from captivity

- Turning the ashes of our life into beauty

- Giving us joy as a replacement for a spirit of oppression

- Rebuilding and reconstructing all elements of our life, including relationships, work and character.

47

He has come to give us life and give it abundantly. As we are walking in His Kingdom, being restored back to life in the Garden of Eden, we will experience this abundance.

B. STAGES OF RESTORATION

We must understand that restoration in our lifetime is not completed until we pass from this life to the next. The process is completed when God creates a new Heaven and a new Earth. We then live eternally in a full state of restoration. Let's look at the stages of this restoration process:

1. *Unbeliever*—These are people remaining spiritually dead, lost and separated from Christ and the Father, with no connection to the reality of the Kingdom.

JOHN 3:16-18

For God so loved the world that He gave His only begotten Son, that whoever believes in Him shall not perish, but have eternal life. For God did not send the Son into the world to judge the world, but that the world might be saved through Him. He who believes in Him is not judged; he who does not believe has been judged already, because he has not believed in the name of the only begotten Son of God.

ROMANS 3:23

For all have sinned and fall short of the glory of God.

ROMANS 6:23

For the wages of sin is death, but the free gift of God is eternal life in Christ Jesus our Lord.

An unbeliever, because he is born with a sin nature without the Spirit of God, stands condemned and separated from any relationship with

God. Without a change in his status (becoming a believer) he will spend eternity condemned and separated from God.

2. *"Born Again" Believer*—This is a spiritually alive, saved member of the Kingdom, with rights and privileges to its benefits.

JOHN 3:3-8

Jesus answered and said to him, "Truly, truly, I say to you, unless one is born again he cannot see the kingdom of God." Nicodemus said to Him, "How can a man be born when he is old? He cannot enter a second time into his mother's womb and be born, can he?" Jesus answered, "Truly, truly, I say to you, unless one is born of water and the Spirit he cannot enter into the kingdom of God. That which is born of the flesh is flesh, and that which is born of the Spirit is spirit. Do not be amazed that I said to you, 'You must be born again.' The wind blows where it wishes and you hear the sound of it, but do not know where it comes from and where it is going; so is everyone who is born of the Spirit."

JOHN 5:24

Truly, truly, I say to you, he who hears My word, and believes Him who sent Me, has eternal life, and does not come into judgment, but has passed out of death into life.

1 JOHN 5:11-12

And the testimony is this; that God has given us eternal life, and this life is in His Son. He who has the Son has the life; he who does not have the Son of God does not have the life. These things I have written to you who believe in the name of the Son of God, so that you may know that you have eternal life.

We (believers) are born again when God places His Spirit within us. We pass at that moment from death into life, because we now have the Son of God within us. Through faith in Him, we are secure in our eternal relationship with God. We actually can begin to experience eternal life now, with a greater experience to come when we move from this earthly existence to a full-time presence with the Father. Don't try to intellectually grasp the way this occurs. It is a spiritual activity that happens outside man's knowledge but within his experiential reality.

3. *Surrendered Believer*—This is a believer who chooses to live the restored and abundant life in the Kingdom.

COLOSSIANS 3:1-17

Therefore if you have been raised up with Christ, keep seeking the things above, where Christ is, seated at the right hand of God. Set your mind on the things above, not on the things that are on earth. For you have died and your life is hidden with Christ in God. When Christ, who is our life, is revealed, then you also will be revealed with Him in glory.

Therefore consider the members of your earthly body as dead to immorality, impurity, passion, evil desire, and greed, which amounts to idolatry. For it is because of these things that the wrath of God will come upon the sons of disobedience, and in them you also once walked, when you were living in them. But now you also, put them all aside: anger, wrath, malice, slander, and abusive speech from your mouth. Do not lie to one another, since you laid aside the old self with its evil practices, and have put on the new self who is being renewed to a true knowledge according to the image of the One who created him—a renewal in which there is no distinction between Greek and Jew, circumcised and uncircumcised, barbarian, Scythian, slave and freeman, but Christ is all, and in all.

So, as those who have been chosen of God, holy and beloved, put on a heart of compassion, kindness, humility, gentleness and patience; bearing with one another, and forgiving each other, whoever has a complaint against anyone; just as the Lord forgave you, so also should you. Beyond all these things put on love, which is the perfect bond of unity. Let the peace of Christ rule in your hearts, to which indeed you were called in one body; and be thankful. Let the word of Christ richly dwell within you, with all wisdom teaching and admonishing one another with psalms and hymns and spiritual songs, singing with thankfulness in your hearts to God. Whatever you do in word or deed, do all in the name of the Lord Jesus, giving thanks through Him to God the Father.

The primary difference between a born again and a surrendered believer is a willingness to be led by the Holy Spirit. He is setting his mind on the things of the Spirit and enjoying the fullness of Kingdom life. This translates into a transformed nature and a life of joy and peace, dwelling richly in and with the Word of God.

4. *Un-surrendered Believer*—This is a believer who, though having accepted Christ as Savior, does not actively seek the Father, and whose life experience begins to parallel that of an unbeliever. Even though he has accepted Christ, he continues to focus on his own and the world's priorities and systems.

HEBREWS 3:15-19

While it is said, "Today if you hear His voice, do not harden your hearts, as when they provoked Me." For who provoked Him when they had heard? Indeed, did not all those who came out of Egypt led by Moses? And with whom was He angry for forty years? Was it not with those who sinned, whose bodies fell in the wilderness? And to whom did He swear that they would not enter His rest, but to those who were disobedient? So we see that they were not able to enter because of unbelief.

DEUTERONOMY 30:11-20

For this commandment, which I command you today, is not too difficult for you, nor is it out of reach. It is not in heaven, that you should say, "Who will go up to heaven for us to get it for us and make us hear it, that we may observe it?" Nor is it beyond the sea, that you should say, "Who will cross the sea for us to get it for us and make us hear it, that we may observe it?" But the word is very near you, in your mouth and in your heart, that you may observe it.

See, I have set before you today life and prosperity, and death and adversity; in that I command you today to love the LORD your God, to walk in His ways and to keep His commandments and His statutes and His judgments, that you may live and multiply, and that the LORD your God may bless you in the land where you are entering to possess it. But if your heart turns away and you will not obey, but are drawn away and worship other gods and serve them, I declare to you today that you shall surely perish. You will not prolong your days in the land where you are crossing the Jordan to enter and possess it. I call heaven and earth to witness against you today, that I have set before you life and death, the blessing and the curse. So choose life in order that you may live, you and your descendants, by loving the LORD your God, by obeying His voice, and by holding fast to Him; for this is your life and the length of your days, that you may live in the land which the LORD swore to your fathers, to Abraham, Isaac, and Jacob, to give them.

ROMANS 8:5-8

For those who are according to the flesh set their minds on the things of the flesh, but those who are according to the Spirit, the things of the Spirit. For the mind set on the flesh is death, but the mind set on the Spirit is life and peace, because the mind set on the flesh is hostile toward God; for it does not subject itself to the law of God, for it is not even able to do so, and those who are in the flesh cannot please God.

The Israelites crossed the Red Sea and were saved. In the New Testament sense, this represents being born again. Having been born again (born-again believers), they were instructed to surrender their will to the Father and cross the Jordan River into the "Promised Land." Jordan in the translated Hebrew literally means "on bended knee" For New Testament believers, the "Promised Land" represents the restored life originally intended in the Garden of Eden. Though instructed by God to cross the Jordan, receive and live in the "Promised Land," the Israelites refused. As a result, they wandered around for forty years. God was angry with them, and they were unable to receive the blessings of the "Promised Land."

We must understand that we, though we are born-again believers, are in the same position. It is possible to wander during our life, outside of God's will, never experiencing the fully restored life because we are unwilling to surrender our life to the Spirit. We instead choose a carnal life in the flesh. The results of this decision are death of the Spirit (quenching the life of the Spirit in us), enmity against God (working my will, at cross-purposes to His will); and inability to please God (wandering around with Him angry at us, not being able to receive the "Promised Land"). We lose the experience of a fully restored life during our time on Earth and the resources of the Kingdom at work.

5. *Heavenly Believer*—A person who is changed at physical death, living in the Heavenly Kingdom in perfect peace, joy and abundance.

PHILIPPIANS 1:21-23

For to me, to live is Christ and to die is gain. But if I am to live on in the flesh, this will mean fruitful labor for me; and I do not know which to choose. But I am hard-pressed from both directions, having the desire to depart and be with Christ, for that is very much better.

2 CORINTHIANS 5:1-5

For we know that if the earthly tent, which is our house, is torn down, we have a building from God, a house not made with hands, eternal in the heavens. For indeed in this house we groan, longing to be clothed with our dwelling from heaven, inasmuch as we, having put it on, will not be found naked. For indeed while we are in this tent, we groan, being burdened, because we do not want to be unclothed but to be clothed, so that what is mortal will be swallowed up by life. Now He who prepared us for this very purpose is God, who gave to us the Spirit as a pledge.

When we pass from this life, we immediately go to be with Christ, translated from our earthly into heavenly bodies. In heaven, there is no sorrow, but joy, peace, and abundance.

1 CORINTHIANS 3:11-23

For no man can lay a foundation other than the one, which is laid, which is Jesus Christ. Now if any man builds on the foundation with gold, silver, precious stones, wood, hay, straw, each man's work will become evident; for the day will show it because it is to be revealed with fire, and the fire itself will test the quality of each man's work. If any man's work, which he has built on it, remains, he will receive a reward. If any man's work is burned up, he will suffer loss; but he himself will be saved, yet so as through fire. Do you not know that you are a temple of God and that the Spirit of God dwells in you? If any man destroys the temple of God, God will destroy him, for the temple of God is holy, and that is what you are.

Let no man deceive himself. If any man among you thinks that he is wise in this age, he must become foolish, so that he may become wise. For the wisdom of this world is foolishness before God. For it is written, "He is the one who catches the wise in their craftiness"; and again, "The Lord knows the reasonings of the wise, that they are useless." So then let no one boast in men. For all things belong to you, whether Paul or Apollos or Cephas or the world or life or death or things present or things to come; all things belong to you, and you belong to Christ; and Christ belongs to God.

It matters whether we have been living our current life as "born again" or as surrendered. It matters, on two levels: here in this life, we will have been wandering around, outside of the will of God, not experiencing the promises of the Covenant or the fully restored, abundant life. In the next life in Heaven, we will be receiving rewards and crowns based upon whether we moved from just being a "born again" believer. Surrendered believers, being led by the Spirit, receive all the Father planned for them.

6. *Eternal Believer*

1 THESSALONIANS 4:13 – 5:11

> *But we do not want you to be uninformed, brethren, about those who are asleep, so that you will not grieve as do the rest who have no hope. For if we believe that Jesus died and rose again, even so God will bring with Him those who have fallen asleep in Jesus. For this we say to you by the word of the Lord, that we who are alive and remain until the coming of the Lord, will not precede those who have fallen asleep. For the Lord Himself will descend from heaven with a shout, with the voice of the archangel and with the trumpet of God, and the dead in Christ will rise first. Then we who are alive and remain will be caught up together with them in the clouds to meet the Lord in the air, and so we shall always be with the Lord. Therefore comfort one another with these words.*
>
> *Now as to the times and the epochs, brethren, you have no need of anything to be written to you. For you yourselves know full well that the day of the Lord will come just like a thief in the night. While they are saying, "Peace and safety!" then destruction will come upon them suddenly like labor pains upon a woman with child, and they will not escape. But you, brethren, are not in darkness, that the day would overtake you like a thief; for you are all sons of light and sons of day. We are not of night nor of darkness; so then let us not sleep as others do, but let us be alert and sober. For those who sleep do their sleeping at night, and those who get drunk get drunk at night. But since we are of the day, let us be sober, having put on the breastplate of faith and love, and as a helmet, the hope of salvation. For God has not destined us for wrath, but for obtaining salvation through our Lord Jesus Christ, who died for us, so that whether we are awake or asleep, we will live together with Him. Therefore encourage one another and build up one another, just as you also are doing.*

At Christ's return, we are either raptured or return with Him in our resurrected bodies, fully restored. We live in a new physical and spiritual dimension as we reign with Him during the millennial period on Earth. At the end of this time, Satan and all demonic forces are completely destroyed and a New Heaven and Earth are created. We live eternally in our fully restored physical and spiritual state as we were always intended to live.

Thus begins the process of restoring the eternal Kingdom of God to its fullness, and we get to join Him in this restoration! As part of this restoration, Earth and Heaven are re-made into the appearance, environment and position God intended at Creation.

SUMMARY

The Kingdom life is an entirely different life than an earthly existence. We see this simply from the changes that occur in our natures as we are reborn and experience a major transformation and renewed way of thinking. Our relationship with the Father now becomes intensely personal and real. We are able to communicate and receive a response. We have access to all He has given us through Christ. We do have a choice to make; we can choose to accept His provision or to stay in a worldly life. That decision determines the nature and experience of our restoration. It can be complete, partial or not even occur. Our desire is to be transformed as completely as possible so as to attain to the "fullness of His glory" and to experience life to the full.

FROM ONE HOME TO ANOTHER—
DEPARTURES AND ARRIVALS

Karen Scott Krone

My husband Bill *loved* trains! His love affair with Lionel began in childhood, when his parents gave him a steam engine with five cars and a caboose. He soon learned how to design a layout, having several trains running in unison. When we married in 1962, an important priority was setting up the trains in the basement of our first home. Vacations were planned around the National Train Collectors' Convention. Bill was definitely a train nut!

In July 2009, Bill was diagnosed with pancreatic cancer. The train obsession took on new importance; he sat at his workbench for hours cleaning and repairing old engines, which seemed to transport him to a place where chemo and cancer were remote. Bill stayed with us for 26 months, much longer than the doctor's prognosis of six to nine months. The trains made the cancer journey more tolerable. On September 14, 2011, Bill slipped quietly from this life into eternity.

At Bill's funeral, our Sunday School teacher, Larry Collett, ended the service with a fitting tribute. Larry said he's often wondered what the journey from earth to God's Kingdom is like. He suggested that for Bill, God arrived with a locomotive to transport him into eternity. Larry painted a beautiful picture with his words: "I can see Bill's eyes light up. I can see him run to the train, excited at what lies ahead and ready to jump aboard with the Conductor." He described Bill's hesitation as he looked back and saw our tear-stained faces, although he knew it was time for him to climb aboard and be transported into God's presence.

Many commented on this wonderful ending to the service. We learned later how God was giving us a memory we would never forget. Bill and I always lived very conservatively; for example, we bought used cars without any frills. It seemed appropriate to do something completely out of character, so I rented a 25-seat Hummer limo to take our large family to the cemetery and on a tour of the important places in Bill's life. The grandchildren loved it! It was amusing to see people stare at this very long limo. Perhaps they were wondering if there was a celebrity behind the dark windows!

We drove by the schools and churches Bill had attended and the homes where he had lived. Our last point of interest was our home of 37 years where our three sons had been raised. The limo stopped in front of the house and we were quiet, letting the memories flood in. Our thoughts included the gigantic train layout in the basement. Suddenly our youngest son, Brad, decided he wanted to meet the people who had been living in "our" home the last eight years. As Brad stepped out of the limo, the new owner, Steve, drove up. He didn't usually come home during the day but he had left some important papers at home. Steve's first thought when he saw the limo was that he had won Publisher's Clearing House! Brad quickly told him who we were and the reason for this unannounced visit. Steve motioned for us to come in, so we all tumbled out of the limo.

He opened the front door and we entered the living room. What an incredible treat for our family to be back in "our" house. Steve was a very gracious and excited host. He said he had a gift for us! How could this be? He had no idea we were coming. We looked at each other, wondering what he was talking about. As he walked toward the garage door he said, "You left something. My wife wanted to pitch it, but I kept it." He disappeared for a minute into the garage and returned with a large painting depicting a train traveling away from us! We were absolutely stunned, and we told Steve about the

analogy we heard at the funeral. It was a very holy moment with tears of gratitude and amazement.

Imagine how many "coincidences" of timing and circumstances had to line up perfectly for us to be so incredibly blessed! Deuteronomy 31:8 says, "The Lord Himself goes before you. He will never leave you nor forsake you." It hasn't been easy living alone without Bill. When life gets difficult, I remember this incredible story and I'm back on the right track of trusting God for the future.

ITEMS TO PONDER

Does your life look restored, considering what you now know about such a life? Have you taken the initial step to allow that to happen and if you have, do you recognize the need the go deeper into a life in the Spirit? Would you prefer the restoration Christ has provided over the results that have been obtained through your own efforts? What are your thoughts?

_____

_____

_____

_____

_____

_____

_____

_____

_____

_____

_____

_____

_____

CHAPTER 5

The Experience of a Restored Life

As young men, we were both very athletic. Rich was a great high school baseball pitcher with ambitions to play professional baseball. He was also an excellent golfer. Larry was selected as one of the two best athletes of his high school class during his senior year. Basketball was his love and he aspired to play at the college level.

As he was acquiring a good record and getting attention from scouts, Rich suddenly began to experience pain in his hip. It would not abate and eventually required medical attention. The diagnosis was a congenital condition, which would only worsen if he continued to play baseball. His athletic career was over.

Larry was attempting to get in shape to try to make his college team as a walk on. He was in the best shape of his life and felt he had a good chance to impress the coaches with his ability. In a workout at the gym, he landed on another player's foot and life was never the same. His knee "blew out" and he could barely walk for two weeks. Without a scholarship, he had no chance to compete in basketball.

Later in life, both men had surgery to partially correct the conditions. Medical techniques were available later to assist in alleviating the problems. Both had to re-focus on a different path in life, entering the world of business. Rich also obtained a theological degree. Since their original plans did not materialize, what would life now become? Both men were devastated at the time of their injuries. As it turned out, it was the best thing that could have happened to both of them. Their lives were eventually restored, but in a much different fashion.

What should we expect from the life in the Kingdom Christ has provided? We know it is a restored and abundant life, but how does that restoration appear? It is one thing to know we have received something, but more important to grasp, recognize and experience its reality. If this has really happened, what can we expect to occur? In this chapter, we will begin to explore the exceptional nature of this experience. In the next chapter we will address more specific blessings and covenantal promises available. A restored life contains the following qualities and characteristics:

WE RECEIVE AND EXPERIENCE WISDOM

The Source of Wisdom

PROVERBS 1:2-7, 23

> To know wisdom and instruction, to discern the sayings of understanding, to receive instruction in wise behavior, righteousness, justice and equity; to give prudence to the naive, to the youth knowledge and discretion, a wise man will hear and increase in learning, and a man of understanding will acquire wise counsel, to understand a proverb and a figure, the words of the wise and their riddles. The fear of the LORD is the beginning of knowledge; fools despise wisdom and instruction…
>
> …Turn to my reproof, behold, I will pour out my spirit on you; I will make my words known to you.

Wisdom is intended to give us the ability to discern and understand God's heart. It requires a desire on our part to hear, learn, and receive

His words. This gives us the ability to make wise decisions about all issues of our lives. This includes understanding righteousness, justice and fairness in all our dealings. God is wisdom and our experience of a restored life allows His wisdom to be transferred to His people.

The Blessing of Wisdom

Proverbs 3:13-18

> *How blessed is the man who finds wisdom and the man who gains understanding. For her profit is better than the profit of silver and her gain better than fine gold. She is more precious than jewels; and nothing you desire compares with her. Long life is in her right hand; in her left hand are riches and honor. Her ways are pleasant ways and all her paths are peace. She is a tree of life to those who take hold of her, and happy are all who hold her fast.*

We will be blessed beyond measure as we understand receiving God's wisdom is more precious than anything we could gain on our own. We will receive blessings and honor. The pace of our day-to-day lives will be pleasant and peaceful. God's wisdom will lead us to a happy life, full of joy and freedom even as we face trials and troubles here on Earth.

The Starting Point for Wisdom

Proverbs 9:10-12

> *The fear of the LORD is the beginning of wisdom and the knowledge of the Holy One is understanding. For, by me, your days will be multiplied, and years of life will be added to you. If you are wise, you are wise for yourself, and if you scoff, you alone will bear it.*

Wisdom begins with the fear of God. This is different from being afraid of God. Rather, it is showing reverence that He is God and we are not. He is eternally spiritual, creator and supreme in all things, and we are His creation. With this kind of fear, we can know everything He speaks, all the promises of His Word and His communications to us are true. If we have a healthy fear of God, we will not debate nor dismiss the promises He speaks. We accept them as truth. Although we may not fully understand, we pursue more wisdom and understanding of how these promises relate to us personally. If we do not have a healthy fear of God and only pursue wisdom on our own, we harm ourselves by living the life of a fool.

The Measure of "Fearing the Lord"

PROVERBS 14:26-27

> *In the fear of the LORD there is strong confidence, and His children will have refuge. The fear of the LORD is a fountain of life, that one may avoid the snares of death.*

As we grow in the fear of the Lord and increase in wisdom, we actually become more sure of our actions, because we gain confidence in seeking, knowing and following the will of God. We come to know His will is best, far better than anything we could desire or have for ourselves.

The Results of Wisdom

PROVERBS 16:20-21

> *He who gives attention to the word will find good, and blessed is he who trusts in the LORD. The wise in heart will be called understanding, and sweetness of speech increases persuasiveness.*

Our role is to pay attention to the word He is speaking to us and recognize His promises are for our good. As we learn to trust in Him through wisdom, we will be blessed and there will be a beauty and sweetness in our conversations. We will be able to communicate the nature and will of God to others.

PROVERBS 19:8, 23

He who gets wisdom loves his own soul; he who keeps understanding will find good…

…The fear of the LORD leads to life, so that one may sleep satisfied, untouched by evil.

As we pursue wisdom, we actually are moving deeper into the restoration process. We discover His goodness. We find satisfaction and rest, and the Lord prevents us from being overwhelmed by evil.

WE EXPERIENCE FREEDOM, PEACE AND JOY

Freedom Brings Transparency

2 CORINTHIANS 3:16-18

But whenever a person turns to the Lord, the veil is taken away. Now the Lord is the Spirit, and where the Spirit of the Lord is, there is liberty. But we all, with unveiled face, beholding as in a mirror the glory of the Lord, are being transformed into the same image from glory to glory, just as from the Lord, the Spirit.

Freedom means true liberty. Liberty is not delayed until we are fully transformed. Transformation is actually a step-by-step process lasting our entire lifetime. It happens during our life journey, as the Lord unveils new things and transforms us, bit by bit, moment by moment.

Freedom Brings Truth

JOHN 8:28-32

So Jesus said, "When you lift up the Son of Man, then you will know that I am He, and I do nothing on My own initiative, but I speak these things as the Father taught Me. And He who sent Me is with Me; He has not left Me alone, for I always do the things that are pleasing to Him. As He spoke these things, many came to believe in Him. So Jesus was saying to those Jews who had believed Him, "If you continue in My word, then you are truly disciples of Mine; and you will know the truth, and the truth will make you free."

As we live the same way Christ lived, doing things that only please the Father, and as we abide (dwell, stay and continue) in His Word, then we will know the truth and understand freedom. Thus we need to develop a passion for abiding in His Word (hearing directly from Him personally) and a passion for truth. This truth is all encompassing: truth about the situation we are currently facing, truth about our heart, truth about others' hearts, and truth that will lead us to freedom. As we develop and maintain this passion, we will experience the fullness of God's freedom and release from the demands of other forces.

Our Environment Changes

ROMANS 14:17

For the Kingdom of God is not eating and drinking, but righteousness and peace and joy in the Holy Spirit.

As we walk in the Holy Spirit in the Kingdom of God, we will be receiving righteousness (the life and nature of Christ himself), peace and joy. It is not dependent upon circumstances. We should understand these traits are indicators of whether or not we're walking in the Kingdom of God. If we are living in peace and joy, we are living in the Kingdom of God. If we are not, we are living in the self and the world, outside the Kingdom. As we realize we are not experiencing peace and joy, this realization should cause us to stop, repent (turn around) and return immediately to His Kingdom, where righteousness peace and joy are fully available, instantaneously.

Our Character Transforms

COLOSSIANS 3:12-17

So, as those who have been chosen of God, holy and beloved, put on a heart of compassion, kindness, humility, gentleness and patience; bearing with one another, and forgiving each other, whoever has a complaint against anyone; just as the Lord forgave you, so also should you. Beyond all these things put on love, which is the perfect bond of unity. Let the peace of Christ rule in your hearts, to which indeed you were called in one body; and be thankful. Let the word of Christ richly dwell within you, with all wisdom teaching and admonishing one another with psalms and hymns and spiritual songs, singing with thankfulness in your hearts to God. Whatever you do in word or deed do all in the name of the Lord Jesus, giving thanks through Him to God the Father.

We will be receiving the very nature of God: compassion, kindness, humility, gentleness, patience, forgiveness toward others, love, etc. Furthermore, we will be receiving God's peace, which rules our life. The word rule, translated from the Greek, means to umpire. Thus we are to let the peace of God act as an umpire in a game. Peace is a determining indicator. If we lack peace, we know we are not walking in the Kingdom of God. The remedy is to repent and return to the Kingdom, where this peace is restored.

WE EXPERIENCE THE EXCEPTIONAL LIFE.

As we are being restored, we will begin experiencing an exceptional life. Let's take a look at this life and how it compares to our current experience.

1. Exceptional authority, victory and power, loosing and binding

GENESIS 1:1-3, 26-28

In the beginning God created the heavens and the earth. The earth was formless and void, and darkness was over the surface of the deep, and the Spirit of God was moving over the surface of the waters. Then God said, "Let there be light"; and there was light....

Then God said, "Let Us make man in Our image, according to Our likeness; and let them rule over the fish of the sea and over the birds of the sky and over the cattle and over all the earth, and over every creeping thing that creeps on the earth." God created man in His own image, in the image of God He created him; male and female He created them. God blessed them; and God said to them, "Be fruitful and multiply, and fill the earth, and subdue it; and rule over the fish of the sea and over the birds of the sky and over every living thing that moves on the earth."

Exceptional authority in the Word means the following: splendor, majesty, beauty, vigor and glory. It also means control, jurisdiction, power to influence; cause to become great and exceedingly abundant. Finally, it is the power (both physical and spiritual) to perform the supernatural. We have been given the right to govern, rule and command, possess authority, perform mighty works, possess great strength, perform miracles, and do all things in excellence.

This was the original intention of God when He created the Garden of Eden and mankind. We were to be co-administrators with Him and have authority over all of His Earth, which He created for us and which He considered to be exceptionally good.

ISAIAH 61:1-4

The Spirit of the Lord GOD is upon me, because the LORD has anointed me to bring good news to the afflicted; He has sent me to bind up the brokenhearted, to proclaim liberty to captives and freedom to prisoners; to proclaim the favorable year of the LORD and the day of vengeance of our God; to comfort all who mourn, to grant those who mourn in Zion, giving them a garland instead of ashes, the oil of gladness instead of mourning, the mantle of praise instead of a spirit of fainting. So they will be called oaks of righteousness, the planting of the LORD, that He may be glorified. Then they will rebuild the ancient ruins, they will raise up the former devastations; and they will repair the ruined cities, the desolations of many generations.

As we experience this authority, we will experience true restoration and transformation, overcoming our sin nature with all of its attached bondage and wounds of oppression. We receive the victory of healing, freedom, release, joy and rebuilding. This superabundant life allows us once again to experience the power of God's authority in our life.

JOHN 10:10

The thief comes only to steal and kill and destroy; I came that they may have life, and have it abundantly.

Countering this provision is the Evil One's desire to keep us from this experience. His goal is to remove "life" from our reality, to take it away and convince us it is not attainable.

2. Exceptional provision

GENESIS 1:28-30

God blessed them; and God said to them, "Be fruitful and multiply, and fill the earth, and subdue it; and rule over the fish of the sea and over the birds of the sky and over every living thing that moves on the earth." Then God said, "Behold, I have given you every plant yielding seed that is on the surface of all the earth, and every tree which has fruit yielding seed; it shall be food for you; and to every beast of the earth and to every bird of the sky and to every thing that moves on the earth which has life, I have given every green plant for food";

and it was so. God saw all that He had made and, behold, it was very good. And there was evening and there was morning, the sixth day.

In the Garden of Eden, God gave every animal, tree, and vegetation for our full provision. He made everything for our use. We would lack nothing. It was all done for our benefit.

PSALMS 23:1-3

The LORD is my shepherd, I shall not want. He makes me lie down in green pastures; He leads me beside quiet waters. He restores my soul; He guides me in the paths of righteousness for His name's sake.

As we walk in the Kingdom and allow the Lord to lead us, we will have this provision. We experience His presence and peace in the beautiful environment He planned, resting in the fullness of His presence. How different this is from the chaos, disorder, noise and stress produced in our earthly abode.

PHILIPPIANS 4:18-20

But I have received everything in full and have it in abundance; I am amply supplied, having received from Epaphroditus what you have sent, a fragrant aroma, an acceptable sacrifice, well pleasing to God. And my God will supply all your needs according to His riches in glory in Christ Jesus. Now to our God and Father be the glory forever and ever. Amen.

God promises to supply all our needs through the provision of Christ Jesus. This is not minimal, but superabundant, as Christ promised in John 10:10. The Father wants us to understand and expect our lives to be full and complete.

3. Exceptional work

GENESIS 2:15

Then the LORD God took the man and put him into the Garden of Eden to cultivate it and keep it.

Before the Fall, God's plan was for mankind to be working in an activity that required skill and abilities. This was to be our occupation and it was always intended to be a pleasant and fulfilling one. Work was not an afterthought or curse, but was to provide the enjoyment of expressing and completing our God-given gifts and abilities.

PSALM 128

How blessed is everyone who fears the LORD, who walks in His ways. When you shall eat of the fruit of your hands, you will be happy and it will be well with you. Your wife shall be like a fruitful vine within your house; your children like olive plants around your table. Behold, for thus shall the man be blessed who fears the LORD. The LORD bless you from Zion, and may you see the prosperity of Jerusalem all the days of your life. Indeed, may you see your children's children. Peace be upon Israel!

Our labor was intended to be a fruitful, joyous and blessed experience. God does not wish our work and work environment to be unhappy and unproductive. If this is the case, we should ask God to restore joy and excitement to our work. We should expect He will improve our work environment or move us to an area where His intention can be received. We should ask Him to restore our work as He restores our life in His Kingdom. We should also consider the condition of our heart, asking God to cleanse it and create enjoyment at work.

ECCLESIASTES 5:18-20; 9:9-10

Here is what I have seen to be good and fitting: to eat, to drink and enjoy oneself in all one's labor in which he toils under the sun during the few years of his life which God has given him; for this is his reward. Furthermore, as for every man to whom God has given riches and wealth, He has also empowered him to eat from them and to receive his reward and rejoice in his labor; this is the gift of God. For he will not often consider the years of his life, because God keeps him occupied with the gladness of his heart...

...Enjoy life with the woman whom you love all the days of your fleeting life which He has given to you under the sun; for this is your reward in life and in your toil in which you have labored under the sun. Whatever your hand finds to do, do it with all your might; for there is no activity or planning or knowledge or wisdom in Sheol where you are going.

We are called to fully enjoy our lives and our work and to realize God is the one who gives us power to create equity, wealth and financial gain from our efforts. Whatever work we have been given, we are to do it to the best of our ability and with enthusiasm, as if the Lord were our employer. Then we will know if it is God's will to remain in our current employment. It should become fulfilling and enjoyable. If not, we need to continue to pursue God's will. He may be moving us to another occupation or place of employment that will be more fulfilling and enjoyable.

4. Exceptional marriage

GENESIS 2:18-25

Then the LORD God said, "It is not good for the man to be alone; I will make him a helper suitable for him." Out of the ground the LORD God formed every beast of the field and every bird of the sky, and brought them to the man to see what he would call them; and whatever the man called a living creature, that was its name. The man gave names to all the cattle, and to the birds of the sky, and to every beast of the field, but for Adam there was not found a helper suitable for him. So the LORD God caused a deep sleep to fall upon the man, and he slept; then He took one of his ribs and closed up the flesh at that place. The LORD God fashioned into a woman the rib, which He had taken from the man, and brought her to the man. The man said, "This is now bone of my bones, and flesh of my flesh; She shall be called Woman, because she was taken out of Man." For this reason a man shall leave his father and his mother and be joined to his wife; and they shall become one flesh. And the man and his wife were both naked and were not ashamed.

Marriage was an institution created by the Father before the Fall. God knows the value and beauty of fellowship and knew that solitude was not beneficial. He created woman so the two of them could become one, in agreement, unity, and harmony. Marriage was always intended to be exceptional. We are to be living with our spouses with great joy and enthusiasm.

PSALM 128

How blessed is everyone who fears the Lord,
When you shall eat of the fruit of your hands,
You will be happy and it will be well with you.
Your wife shall be like a fruitful vine within your house,
Your children like olive plants around your table.
Behold, for thus shall the man be blessed who fears the Lord.
The Lord bless you from Zion, and may you see the prosperity of Jerusalem
all the days of your life.
Indeed, may you see your children's, children.
Peace be upon Israel!

There is nothing better than enjoying our marriage and family, having fellowship as if every day were Thanksgiving. When our marriages and families are thriving, we are truly blessed.

PSALM 133

Behold, how good and how pleasant it is for brothers to dwell together in unity! It is like the precious oil upon the head, coming down upon the beard, Even Aaron's beard, coming down upon the edge of his robes. It is like the dew of Hermon coming down upon the mountains of Zion; for there the LORD commanded the blessing—life forever.

Unity with spouses is one of God's principles for our lives. When we are experiencing unity in marriage, we will be truly blessed, and God will, in fact, command blessing upon us. This is one of the amazing benefits of a restored life. Our marriages can truly be exceptional, filled with unity, and receptive to the blessings God is commanding. What more could we ever desire or expect from marriage?

5. Exceptional identity

GENESIS 1:26-27, 31

Then God said, "Let Us make man in Our image, according to Our likeness; and let them rule over the fish of the sea and over the birds of the sky and over the cattle and over all the earth, and over every creeping thing that creeps on the earth." God created man in His own image, in the image of God He created him; male and female He created them…

…God saw all that He had made, and behold it was very good. And there was evening and there was morning, the sixth day.

Since we are created in God's image, we are identified as His children and family, reflecting His likeness. God considers us to be exceptionally good, valuable and very precious. Being made in God's image means others see Him through us. As we live the restored life, we are transformed more and more into His image. As we walk with Him, we begin to think and act more like Him. No other creature but man has that ability.

74

Psalm 16

Preserve me, O God, for I take refuge in You. I said to the Lord, "You are my Lord; I have no good besides You."

As for the saints who are in the earth, They are the majestic ones in whom is all my delight. The sorrows of those who have bartered for another god will be multiplied; I shall not pour out their drink offerings of blood, Nor will I take their names upon my lips.

The Lord is the portion of my inheritance and my cup; You support my lot. The lines have fallen to me in pleasant places; Indeed, my heritage is beautiful to me. I will bless the Lord who has counseled me; indeed, my mind instructs me in the night. I have set the Lord continually before me; Because He is at my right hand, I will not be shaken. Therefore my heart is glad and my glory rejoices; My flesh also will dwell securely. For You will not abandon my soul to Sheol; Nor will You allow Your Holy One to undergo decay.

You will make known to me the path of life; In Your presence is fullness of joy; In Your right hand, there are pleasures forever.

The Psalmist says we are God's majesty, in whom He delights. He desires us to have a pleasant environment and to know we are beautiful and precious to Him. We are to have glad and joyful hearts as we experience the fullness of His presence and His everlasting security and protection. He freely wishes to give these, because we are His children and are walking in the Kingdom.

6. Exceptional communion with God

Genesis 3:8-11

They heard the sound of the LORD God walking in the garden in the cool of the day, and the man and his wife hid themselves from the presence of the LORD God among the trees of the garden. Then the LORD God called to the man, and said to him, "Where are you?" He said, "I heard the sound of You in the garden, and I was afraid because I was naked; so I hid myself." And He said, "Who told you that you were naked? Have you eaten from the tree of which I commanded you not to eat?"

In the restored Kingdom life, close communion with the Father is again available. We can have perfect communion with God and are able to experience His presence, communicate directly with Him and understand what is on His heart and mind. He also walks with us, knows our heart's desires and communicates freely.

PSALM 95

O come, let us sing for joy to the Lord, let us shout joyfully to the rock of our salvation. Let us come before His presence with thanksgiving, let us shout joyfully to Him with psalms. For the Lord is a great God and a great King above all gods, in whose hand are the depths of the earth, the peaks of the mountains are His also. The sea is His, for it was He who made it, and His hands formed the dry land. Come, let us worship and bow down, let us kneel before the Lord our Maker. For He is our God, and we are the people of His pasture and the sheep of His hand. Today, if you would hear His voice, do not harden your hearts, as at Meribah, as in the day of Massah in the wilderness, "When your fathers tested Me, They tried Me, though they had seen My work. For forty years I loathed that generation, and said they are a people who err in their heart, And they do not know My ways. Therefore I swore in My anger, truly they shall not enter into My rest."

As we come before God's presence with thanksgiving and joy, we understand we are His, the people of His Kingdom and His children. As a result, today, at this moment, He will speak to us, and we will have the ability to hear Him. As we understand our true identity, we will not become rebellious by testing Him (asking Him to prove himself before we pursue obedience). Instead we will maintain humble hearts and enjoy the privilege of hearing His voice.

JOHN 10:3-5, 27-30

To him the doorkeeper opens, and the sheep hear his voice, and he calls his own sheep by name and leads them out. When he puts forth all his own, he goes ahead of them, and the sheep follow him because they know his voice. A stranger they simply will not follow, but will flee from him, because they do not know the voice of strangers...

...My sheep hear My voice, and I know them, and they follow Me; and I give eternal life to them, and they will never perish; and no one will snatch them out of My hand. My Father, who has given them to Me, is greater than all; and no one is able to snatch them out of the Father's hand. I and the Father are one.

One of the indicators we are living in the Kingdom is our ability to hear His voice. The enemy's voice or the voices of the world do not confuse us. Instead, we hear clearly because we are developing special communion and discerning His distinct voice. He knows us and desires to speak to us. We are to willingly follow all He speaks.

SUMMARY

Do we desire our lives to be wise, peaceful and exceptional? Of course we do! The problem is, we define peace or wisdom in the context of an earthly existence. However, we subsequently discover that definition is incorrect. All the models of earthly exceptionalism, which rely on our performance or achievement, never bring forth the anticipated results. While we can grasp this paradox intellectually, we need to grapple with the possibility of an alternative.

When we understand and pursue what God has provided through Christ, we learn we can have a full and satisfying life experience. When we delve deeply into the attributes of this life, we find it not only differs from a secular, worldly model, but also promises and delivers much more. Where else can we receive the quantity and quality of life the

Father delivers? What else could we truly desire? What else can satisfy our most heartfelt desires? When we realize the fullness of life in Christ, our mind can begin to adjust the focus and alignment of our activities, and our character can be conformed to that of the King.

REFLECTION

In order to experience the restored life, we need wisdom. Since it only comes from the Father, do I really understand how I must seek it in order to receive it? Is my life characterized by freedom, peace and joy? What should I be doing in order for this to be more and more present? Do I consider my life to be exceptional? Am I experiencing the abundance of provision God's word says He wants to provide? Is my marriage and work experience demonstrating a restored life?

When we understand what God has made available through Christ, we realize how our lives lack the fulfillment intended by the Father. In the space below, describe how you would like these areas to improve and what you sense the Father wants you to experience.

CHAPTER 6

The Blessings
of a Restored Life

After reflecting on the previous chapter, what could be a greater blessing than wisdom, freedom, peace, joy and the exceptionality of a restored life? It is hard to believe there is even more available for the believer. Well, there is! Life in the Father brings a whole different dimension. It reconnects us with the original intentions the Father desired at creation. We now have access to everything, and the complete package is far greater than we could ever imagine. In this chapter, we want to look at the blessings, promises, direction, success and fellowship that have been made available through Christ. Do our lives mirror these? If not, look what can lie ahead. We begin to see what Jesus meant when He said He came to give us an abundant life.

THE COVENANT

The covenant is an agreement between God and his followers, each meeting their side of the agreement. God's covenant is everlasting and always available to us. God is faithful to fulfill His side of the agreement and the stipulations of the covenant still stand today for believers.

The Blessing

GENESIS 12:1-3

Now the LORD said to Abram, "Go forth from your country, and from your relatives and from your father's house to the land which I will show you; and I will make you a great nation, and I will bless you and make your name great; and so you shall be a blessing; and I will bless those who bless you, and the one who curses you I will curse. And in you all the families of the earth will be blessed."

God's covenant with Abraham began when He promised to bless Abraham and make him a blessing (so he would receive the blessing and subsequently give it to others). This is the essence of the covenant, which still stands today. God promises to bless us and to make our lives a blessing to others. This wonderful covenant operates when we are walking in the Spirit, walking in His Kingdom and fully surrendered to Him. Some of the major elements of this Covenant are discussed below.

Enduring

GENESIS 17:1-8

Now when Abram was ninety-nine years old, the LORD appeared to Abram and said to him, "I am God Almighty; Walk before Me, and be blameless. I will establish My covenant between Me and you, and I will multiply you exceedingly." Abram fell on his face, and God talked with him, saying, "As for Me, behold, My covenant is with you, and you will be the father of a multitude of nations. No longer shall your name be called Abram, but your name shall be Abraham; for I will make you the father of a multitude of nations. I will make you exceedingly fruitful, and I will make nations of you, and kings will come forth from you. I will establish My covenant between Me and you and your descendants after you throughout their generations for an everlasting covenant, to be God to you and to your descendants after you. I will give to you and to your descendants after you, the land of your sojournings, all the land of Canaan, for an everlasting possession; and I will be their God.

In order for us to receive the blessings of the covenant (that He will multiply and bless us exceedingly and abundantly), we must walk with Him and be blameless. Being blameless is not performing perfectly, but letting the righteousness of Christ's nature become ours. We are covered by His holiness. This Covenant is an everlasting covenant and moves from generation to generation. We are still part of the generations receiving the Covenant.

Abundant

DEUTERONOMY 28:1-15

Now it shall be, if you diligently obey the Lord your God, being careful to do all His commandments which I command you today, the Lord your God will set you high above all the nations of the earth. All these blessings will come upon you and overtake you if you obey the Lord your God: Blessed shall you be in the city, and blessed shall you be in the country. Blessed shall be the offspring of your body and the produce of your ground and the offspring of your beasts, the increase of your herd and the young of your flock. Blessed shall be your basket and your kneading bowl. Blessed shall you be when you come in, and blessed shall you be when you go out. The Lord shall cause your enemies who rise up against you to be defeated before you; they will come out against you one way and will flee before you seven ways. The Lord will command the blessing upon you in your barns and in all that you put your hand to, and He will bless you in the land which the Lord your God gives you. The Lord will establish you as a holy people to Himself, as He swore to you, if you keep the commandments of the Lord your God and walk in His ways. So all the peoples of the earth will see that you are called by the name of the Lord, and they will be afraid of you. The Lord will make you abound in prosperity, in the offspring of your body and in the offspring of your beast and in the produce of your ground, in the land which the Lord swore to your fathers to give you. The Lord will open for you His good storehouse, the heavens, to give rain to your land in its season and to bless all the work of your hand; and you shall lend to many nations, but you shall not borrow. The Lord will make you the head and not the tail, and you only will be above, and you will not be underneath, if you listen to the commandments of the Lord your God, which I charge you today, to observe them carefully, and do not turn aside from any of the words which I command you today, to the right or to the left, to go after other gods to serve them. But it shall come about, if you do not obey the Lord your God, to observe to do all His commandments and His statutes with which I charge you today, that all these curses will come upon you and overtake you."

In order for us to receive the blessings of the Covenant, we must hear God's instruction and willingly follow it. The promised blessings are numerous. Our enemies will be defeated. God will command His blessings upon our resources and provide financial security. Our work will flourish. We will not have to borrow, but will be in a position of leadership and independence. We fully receive this covenant from God Almighty when we are walking in the Kingdom under His rule. However if we do not follow what He instructs (or even fail to listen), the consequences are serious. They appear in the form of curses, which withhold the promised blessings and allow us to suffer the consequences of not being protected by the Kingdom. This is because we are walking only in the powers of self and the world.

Our Requirement

a. Serve the Father

DEUTERONOMY 10:12-14

Now, Israel, what does the LORD your God require from you, but to fear the LORD your God, to walk in all His ways and love Him, and to serve the LORD your God with all your heart and with all your soul, and to keep the

LORD's commandments and His statutes which I am commanding you today
for your good? Behold, to the LORD your God belong heaven and the highest
heavens, the earth and all that is in it.

The covenant requirements for us are clear. We are to fear the Lord
(have awe and reverence for God Almighty) knowing that all He
speaks, including these covenant promises, is true. We should walk
with Him, remaining in the Kingdom, and love Him. Our desire
should be for an intimate relationship with Him. Finally, we are to
serve Him, surrendering our will to His and completely obeying His
instructions to us.

b. Choose Life

DEUTERONOMY 30:11-20

"For this commandment, which I command you today is not too difficult for
you, nor is it out of reach. It is not in heaven, that you should say, 'Who will
go up to heaven for us to get it for us and make us hear it, that we may observe
it?' Nor is it beyond the sea, that you should say, 'Who will cross the sea for
us to get it for us and make us hear it, that we may observe it?' But the word
is very near you, in your mouth and in your heart, that you may observe it.

"See, I have set before you today life and prosperity, and death and adversity;
in that I command you today to love the Lord your God, to walk in His ways
and to keep His commandments and His statutes and His judgments, that you
may live and multiply, and that the Lord your God may bless you in the land
where you are entering to possess it. But if your heart turns away and you will
not obey, but are drawn away and worship other gods and serve them, I declare
to you today that you shall surely perish. You will not prolong your days in the
land where you are crossing the Jordan to enter and possess it. I call heaven
and earth to witness against you today, that I have set before you life and death,
the blessing and the curse. So choose life in order that you may live, you and
your descendants, by loving the Lord your God, by obeying His voice, and by

holding fast to Him; for this is your life and the length of your days, that you may live in the land which the Lord swore to your fathers, to Abraham, Isaac, and Jacob, to give them."

Since the Father stands eternally behind His covenant with Abraham and desires to bless us with its full provision, He makes it very simple for us to decide. It is not so complicated that we need somebody more mature to explain it. Rather it is God, Himself, who declares the alternatives. It is our choice. If we choose to follow Him, remaining in His Kingdom we will be recipients of blessings in our lives. If we choose not to follow Him and walk on our own, outside of the Kingdom, we will suffer the consequences.

PROMISES OF HIS WORD (RHEMA) TO US

As we walk with the Father in the Kingdom, under His rule, He speaks His promises directly to us. The Greek word for God speaking His word to us is "Rhema." Our life is not intended to be a "name it and claim it" system, which is really operating in the self, since our wills would be dictating our lives. By definition, that places us outside the Kingdom and in the control of the world. But if we are walking in the Kingdom of God, the promises are all available, to be received as He speaks specifically to us. Let's examine what Scripture says about the promises of God and what we can expect as God speaks these to us personally.

They are Firm

2 Corinthians 1:18-24

But as God is faithful, our word to you is not yes and no. For the Son of God, Christ Jesus, who was preached among you by us-by me and Silvanus and Timothy—was not yes and no, but is yes in Him. For as many as are the promises of God, in Him they are yes; therefore also through Him is our Amen to the glory of God through us. Now He who establishes us with you in Christ and anointed us is God, who also sealed us and gave us the Spirit in our hearts as a pledge. But I call God as witness to my soul, that to spare you I did not come again to Corinth. Not that we lord it over your faith, but are workers with you for your joy; for in your faith you are standing firm.

All the promises of God are "yes" in Christ Jesus. This is critical since God does not play favorites. Thus, His promises are not perhaps or maybe, but are always **yes**. We can count on Him fulfilling His promises. The simple condition is we remain in Christ, in the Kingdom and walking in the Spirit. When we are in Christ, we will be receiving promises given specifically to us, and we can count on them being absolute and true.

They are Transmitted

JOHN 15:7-8

If you abide in Me, and My words abide in you, ask whatever you wish, and it will be done for you. My Father is glorified by this, that you bear much fruit, and so prove to be My disciples.

As we abide in Him, hearing His voice, receiving His instruction and promises, and being obedient to Him, we can pray these promises and fully expect them to be performed. This expectation is just one of the many blessings that are experienced through our abiding. The Father wants to show us, in the world, that He is God Almighty and circumstances can be altered. Supernatural, miraculous solutions (through His promises) can be experienced and serve to bear witness to our walking in His Kingdom.

DIRECTION (His Path)

In order for us to walk in the Kingdom, we must follow His specific path for us. The path is unique and directed by the vinedresser (the Father) as He walks us through life. Since we are called to follow His path for us, He must communicate directly to us and guide our steps.

As we walk in the Kingdom, the King directly reveals to us the best possible way to receive His blessings and to experience the fullness of His Kingdom. Let's delve deeper into God promises about directing our steps and the conditions for this to occur.

Remembering, Recording and Trusting

PROVERBS 3:1-6

> *My son, do not forget my teaching, but let your heart keep my commandments; for length of days and years of life and peace they will add to you. Do not let kindness and truth leave you; bind them around your neck, write them on the tablet of your heart. So you will find favor and good repute in the sight of God and man. Trust in the LORD with all your heart and do not lean on your own understanding. In all your ways acknowledge Him, and He will make your paths straight.*

As we internalize His instruction to us (in our heart), live in kindness and pursue truth, we find favor and good reputation from God and those around us. We recall His instruction as we fully trust in Him, not depending on our own knowledge or perception. When we cease striving to "figure things out" by ourselves or limiting ourselves only to what we can understand, the Lord will provide direction and clarity.

Surrendering

PROVERBS 16:9

> *The mind of man plans his way, but the LORD directs his steps.*

It is easy for us to rationally make our own decisions, but it is better to surrender our will to the Father and allow Him to direct our activity. Essentially, we place His word and desires above our own intellect, rationale and knowledge.

Following

PROVERBS 20:24

Man's steps are ordained by the LORD. How then can man understand his way?

It is important to follow God's leading whether or not we fully understand. Because His thoughts often contradict ours, we cannot always see how He is drawing us into His greater Kingdom story. We are simply called to allow Him to lead us and to be obedient to His direction.

SUCCESS

The Hebrew word for success literally means "to prosper through having wisdom and knowing which way to go". Success means we will be free of the burdens of life and be at rest. It does not necessarily equate to wealth, but rather freedom manifested in our lifestyle. Thus, a farmer in Africa can be as "successful" as a wealthy executive in the United States. Since God is not partial, this promise of success is available to all. Some of the elements of this success are:

Ability to Prevail

JOSHUA 1:5-8

No man will be able to stand before you all the days of your life. Just as I have been with Moses, I will be with you; I will not fail you or forsake you. Be strong and courageous, for you shall give this people possession of the land which I swore to their fathers to give them. Only be strong and very courageous; be careful to do according to all the law which Moses My servant commanded you; do not turn from it to the right or to the left, so that you may have success wherever you go. This book of the law shall not depart from your mouth, but you shall meditate on it day and night, so that you may be careful

to do according to all that is written in it; for then you will make your way
prosperous, and then you will have success.

The promise of success includes the enemy's inability to prevail against us. God will never leave us nor abandon us; He does not fail. We can have success in all things and He can bring prosperity into our lives. The key is meditating on the word of God. This means staying in intimate communication with God regarding His word to us until it becomes planted in our heart and we believe it to be true.

Long-Term in Nature

Psalm 1

How blessed is the man who does not walk in the counsel of the wicked,
Nor stand in the path of sinners, nor sit in the seat of scoffers! But his delight
is in the law of the Lord, and in His law he meditates day and night. He
will be like a tree firmly planted by streams of water, which yields its fruit in
its season and its leaf does not wither; And in whatever he does, he prospers.
The wicked are not so. But they are like chaff, which the wind drives away.
Therefore the wicked will not stand in the judgment, Nor sinners in the
assembly of the righteous. For the Lord knows the way of the righteous, but
the way of the wicked will perish.

Our prosperity and success will be long-lasting. We will be like trees that consistently receive water (the life and power of the Holy Spirit), resulting in fruit (answered prayer according to God's will) and the promised prosperity in all we do. We must avoid taking direction and instruction from those who are not walking in the Kingdom. We should delight in abiding in the word of God, meditating on His Rhema word of instruction and His promises to us.

KOINONIA (Community & Fellowship)

God does not want us to live a life independent of one another, but to be an interdependent part of the Body of Christ, walking in the Spirit and in the Kingdom of God. This community and fellowship with other Spirit-filled believers, each surrendering their will to God and walking in His Kingdom, provides strength and assistance in hearing His will and having our paths directed by Him. It also fulfills the need for fellowship and camaraderie with others. We share life together, serve as partners, seek God's best for each other, and become friends in the process.

Our Fellowship is Grounded in Christ and the Father

1 JOHN 1:1-7

> *What was from the beginning, what we have heard, what we have seen with our eyes, what we have looked at and touched with our hands, concerning the Word of Life—and the life was manifested, and we have seen and testify and proclaim to you the eternal life, which was with the Father and was manifested to us—what we have seen and heard we proclaim to you also, so that you too may have fellowship with us; and indeed our fellowship is with the Father, and with His Son Jesus Christ. These things we write, so that our joy may be made complete. This is the message we have heard from Him and announce to you, that God is Light, and in Him there is no darkness at all. If we say that we have fellowship with Him and yet walk in the darkness, we lie and do not practice the truth; but if we walk in the Light as He Himself is in the Light, we have fellowship with one another, and the blood of Jesus His Son cleanses us from all sin.*

Our fellowship is not merely between other persons, but together with the Father, Son and Holy Spirit. If we walk in the light (together walking in His Kingdom) we are privileged to experience fellowship with each other and to be separated from our worldly nature. We are

91

transformed into our Kingdom nature and provide support for each other in this process.

It is Expressed and Demonstrated in Community

ACTS 2:40-47

> *And with many other words he solemnly testified and kept on exhorting them, saying, "Be saved from this perverse generation"! So then, those who had received his word were baptized; and that day there were added about three thousand souls. They were continually devoting themselves to the apostles' teaching and to fellowship, to the breaking of bread and to prayer. Everyone kept feeling a sense of awe; and many wonders and signs were taking place through the apostles. And all those who had believed were together and had all things in common; and they began selling their property and possessions and were sharing them with all, as anyone might have need. Day by day continuing with one mind in the temple, and breaking bread from house to house, they were taking their meals together with gladness and sincerity of heart, praising God and having favor with all the people. And the Lord was adding to their number day by day those who were being saved.*

After three thousand people, at Pentecost, responded to the call from Peter to accept Christ, they began gathering in homes (small groups) to experience life together. They were abiding in the word, staying in intimate community, communing with God, praying and having dialogue with God. They remained in a state of reverence and awe (fear of God) and they experienced amazing wonders and signs. They witnessed the fulfillment of God's supernatural promises to them. There was fellowship in experiencing signs and wonders and bearing witness to others. Life in the Kingdom was real and very attractive. As a result, people turned to Christ every day, joined the fellowship and entered the Kingdom of God.

SUMMARY

Life as initially created by the Father was intended to receive all the blessings He provided. The Father, through Christ, has now made this available again. His definition of success is clearly different from that of the world. Jesus knew this and was steadfast in doing the Father's work. One could say He walked to the tune of a different "drummer." So can we! It is important to know the leader and to follow His direction. We can expect to receive the Father's covenant promises and have experiences and relationships unknown to the secular world. Because many have not had that experience, they have reduced their expectations to those of the world. As a result, they fail to receive the wondrous blessings the Father has made available.

We should not allow our focus on Christ and the promises of Scripture to be become secondary to worldly activity. That is why Jesus told us to "seek first the Kingdom of God." The Kingdom has to be preeminent. Keeping Him at the center of our life is necessary. The blessings arise from staying engaged with Him. Simply because others have not had a Kingdom experience should not deter us from avidly seeking the Father and His Kingdom.

In his book *On China*, Henry Kissinger relates an ancient Chinese fable called "The Foolish Old Man Who Removed the Mountains." The story describes a man who lived in the mountains of northern China and whose home faced south. There were two mountains that stood in the way of a perfect view and easy access. He and his sons began to dig up these mountains. A local "wise man" derided and criticized them for starting such an impossible task. The man responded, "When I die my sons will carry on; when they die, there will be my grandsons, and then their sons and grandsons, and so on to infinity. High as they are, the mountains cannot grow any higher and with every bit we dig, they will be that much lower. Why can't we clear them away?"

So should our perspective be on the work of the Father. We should expect it to occur regardless of any obstacles, circumstances or time parameters. If the Father declares something, we should anticipate it will happen. And, we should live in a manner that awaits and encourages its reality.

WATER INTO WINE?

We were having our annual leaders' retreat for Living Waters Ministry. This spring's gathering was in the wine country of California. It was truly spectacular as the Lord led us to a much deeper place in understanding we are living in both heaven and earth and have received every spiritual blessing in the heavenly places in Christ. Furthermore, we studied how we have been raised with Him and are sitting at the right hand of the Father with Christ. It was a very profound time as we unpacked these truths and understood how they applied to us personally as He spoke to each one in attendance. We could all say that our level of revelation was heightened beyond anything we had previously experienced. It was great!

During our free time in the afternoon, Neal and Kathy Weisenberger arranged for a tasting at a local boutique winery owned by Christian friends of theirs. They took us on a tour of the vineyard and God revealed more things about abiding, along with revelation received about adversity. The owners shared openly about how they abide in the Word and how beautiful their life was because of this abiding relationship. We were thrilled at God reinforcing the true meaning of abiding (not just studying, but remaining 24/7 in relationship, centered on abiding in the word). One of our attendees had e-mailed me during the retreat that the Lord had asked him to have me spend time with our leaders clarifying this truth. We all tend to drift into the mindset of just studying. We had numerous opportunities to process this truth as He spoke to us. The vineyard owners are called "dry farmers," who rely completely on the weather for rain and frost prevention in order to protect the vineyard and have a bountiful and fruitful crop.

However, the area where this vineyard resides had only received two inches of rain this season, when normally they would have received about thirty. We drove by reservoirs and saw firsthand they were almost dry. The owners said if they did not receive rain soon, their crop could be completely destroyed and they would be out of business. Based on what we were learning about living in heaven and earth and the supernatural work of God, we said, "Let's ask the Father and pray that He send rain. So we prayed! Later that day, the owner e-mailed me and thanked me for bringing Living Waters to her vineyard. It had been such a blessing to her. She heard God say yes, He was answering her prayers. She said she was going out and buying the biggest umbrella she could find, as she believed what He said.

On Sunday morning, we woke up to a soaking rain that lasted all day. It was not forecasted. She told me later that evening she was overwhelmed and attributed it all to the glory of God. It was exactly what was needed to save the vineyard. Later in the week, there were news articles about the unusual nature of this Sunday's rain. There was a lack of understanding how it happened. But we knew! Northern California received much-needed moisture all that week and the mountains (that had minimal snow) were deluged with accumulation. We were privileged to see firsthand that heaven is here, as we live in this dual dimension of God's life, and nothing is too difficult for Him.

REFLECTION

The restored life is filled with great blessings promised by the Father. Can we even imagine what our lives would be if we were receiving just a small portion of these promises? In what ways do you see these blessings missing in your life? Are you willing to take the steps necessary to have your life characterized by the blessings and promises discussed in this chapter? Write down some of the items you would like to experience more often and how it would change the current direction of your life.

_____

_____

_____

_____

_____

_____

_____

_____

_____

_____

_____

CHAPTER 7

The Production of Fruit

THE ESSENCE OF "FRUIT"

GALATIANS 5:22-23

> *But the fruit of the Spirit is love, joy, peace, patience, kindness, goodness, faithfulness, gentleness, self-control; against such things there is no law.*

JOHN 15:7-8

> *If you abide in Me, and My words abide in you, ask whatever you wish, and it will be done for you. My Father is glorified by this, that you bear much fruit, and so prove to be My disciples.*

Bearing fruit is central to our life in Christ. It needs to be a constant experience if we are sharing the reality of a Kingdom life.

HOW FRUIT IS PRODUCED

God's fruit is being produced in our life. It is His fruit, produced through abiding, and not created on our own (remember, we can do nothing apart from Christ). There are two fundamental types of fruit. First there is the transformation of our soul, when by His work our sinful nature becomes our new nature and begins to reflect the fruits of the Spirit. Then there is the fulfillment of His will, where God changes circumstances and performs supernatural works. Only He can do this. It is important to understand not only how fruit is produced, but to grasp its qualities and benefits.

It is part of our life purpose

JOHN 15:16

> *You did not choose Me but I chose you, and appointed you that you would go and bear fruit, and that your fruit would remain, so that whatever you ask of the Father in My name He may give to you.*

We are appointed to produce fruit. He has chosen us for the very purpose of bearing fruit according to His plan. This fruit will not wither and die, but will remain and endure.

It is part of our "new life" in Christ.

ROMANS 7:4

> *Therefore, my brethren, you also were made to die to the Law through the body of Christ, so that you might be joined to another, to Him who was raised from the dead, in order that we might bear fruit for God.*

Spiritual fruit is a product of the resurrection. We are joined with Him in resurrected life for the purpose of having His resurrected power active in our lives and to produce His desired fruit.

It is "aligned" with the Father

COLOSSIANS 1:9-12

> *For this reason also, since the day we heard of it, we have not ceased to pray for you and to ask that you may be filled with the knowledge of His will in all spiritual wisdom and understanding, so that you will walk in a manner worthy of the Lord, to please Him in all respects, bearing fruit in every good work and increasing in the knowledge of God; strengthened with all power,*

according to His glorious might, for the attaining of all steadfastness and patience; joyously giving thanks to the Father, who has qualified us to share in the inheritance of the saints in Light.

In the passage above, "knowledge" means experience and intimate life, not head knowledge. Fruit is the evidence of a life committed to God. We bear fruit through joining Him in the good works He has undertaken. In addition to fruit being produced, our personal experience of the Father will increase and deepen.

It is continuous, not seasonal

PSALM 92:12-15

The righteous man will flourish like the palm tree. He will grow like a cedar in Lebanon. Planted in the house of the LORD, they will flourish in the courts of our God. They will still yield fruit in old age; they shall be full of sap and very green, to declare that the LORD is upright; He is my rock, and there is no unrighteousness in Him.

Bearing fruit does not cease with age and continues for eternity. It is not intended for us to only occasionally bear fruit. We are to bear fruit throughout our years on Earth. It is not dependent on our physical age, but on our spiritual relationship with God. This fruit is not temporal, but eternal. It lasts forever.

EZEKIEL 47:12

By the river on its bank, on one side and on the other, will grow all kinds of trees for food. Their leaves will not wither and their fruit will not fail. They will bear every month because their water flows from the sanctuary, and their fruit will be for food and their leaves for healing.

We are able to bear an abundance of fruit. There is continuous output. There are no seasons or limiting factors to the production of fruit. This is because the Father is producing it. Neither is there any limit to His ability to use the fruit.

It emanates through righteousness.

EPHESIANS 5:8-12

> *Walk as children of Light (for the fruit of the Light consists in all goodness and righteousness and truth), trying to learn what is pleasing to the Lord. Do not participate in the unfruitful deeds of darkness, but instead even expose them; for it is disgraceful even to speak of the things, which are done by them in secret.*

Fruit is always good, right and true. It is God's work creating evidence of His glory, not ours. It will always be based on and bear witness to His truth.

It is excellent (exceptional)

PHILIPPIANS 1:9-11

> *And this I pray, that your love may abound still more and more in real knowledge and all discernment, so that you may approve the things that are excellent, in order to be sincere and blameless until the day of Christ; having been filled with the fruit of righteousness which comes through Jesus Christ, to the glory and praise of God.*

Just as fruit requires large amounts of sunlight to grow and prosper, we need the goodness and truthfulness of the Father for it to be displayed. The light in which we grow and bear fruit is the Father.

THE CHARACTERISTICS OF FRUIT

Fruit is produced, created and completed, as we abide in the "Vine". This relationship is comparable to the original "tree of life" in the Garden of Eden. The "tree" was meant to be the source of all abundant, exceptional life. So is our abiding relationship with the Father. Let's examine how it actually takes form and directly benefits our lives.

It is part of our intended "being."

GENESIS 1:29-31; 2:8-9

> Then God said, "Behold, I have given you every plant yielding seed that is on the surface of all the earth, and every tree which has fruit yielding seed; it shall be food for you; and to every beast of the earth and to every bird of the sky and to every thing that moves on the earth which has life, I have given every green plant for food"; and it was so. God saw all that He had made, and behold, it was very good. And there was evening and there was morning, the sixth day…

> …The LORD God planted a garden toward the east, in Eden; and there He placed the man whom He had formed. Out of the ground the LORD God caused to grow every tree that is pleasing to the sight and good for food; the tree of life also in the midst of the garden, and the tree of the knowledge of good and evil.

The "tree of life" was given to provide all the "food" that mankind would need. The fruit we enjoy is not just an outcome, but provides sustenance as well. It will actually contribute to all we need, particularly for our spiritual growth and maturity.

It is covered in wisdom.

PROVERBS 3:13-24

> How blessed is the man who finds wisdom
> And the man who gains understanding.
> For her profit is better than the profit of silver
> And her gain better than fine gold.
> She is more precious than jewels;
> And nothing you desire compares with her.

Long life is in her right hand;
In her left hand are riches and honor.
Her ways are pleasant ways
And all her paths are peace.
She is a tree of life to those who take hold of her,
And happy are all who hold her fast.
The Lord by wisdom founded the earth,
By understanding He established the heavens.
By His knowledge the deeps were broken up
And the skies drip with dew.
My son let them not vanish from your sight;
Keep sound wisdom and discretion,
So they will be life to your soul
And adornment to your neck.
Then you will walk in your way securely
And your foot will not stumble.
When you lie down, you will not be afraid;
When you lie down, your sleep will be sweet.

This fruit is wisdom (from God). It provides direction. We can live a pleasant life of peace and security, free from fear and full of the serenity and joy of the Kingdom. Wisdom also emanates from the "tree of life". Therefore, it is fruit, which is available for our consumption.

It is flourishing

PROVERBS 11:27-30

He who diligently seeks good seeks favor, but he who seeks evil, evil will come to him. He who trusts in his riches will fall, but the righteous will flourish like the green leaf. He who troubles his own house will inherit wind and the foolish will be servant to the wise hearted. The fruit of the righteous is a tree of life, and he who is wise wins souls.

Fruit is receiving favor and flourishing. When we seek the righteousness of God (by staying in the Kingdom), we can expect the favor of God to be evidenced in our lives. Even if it may seem absent at times, the Father will not fail to take us deeper into His Kingdom and allow us to experience life in a more meaningful way.

It is fulfillment

PROVERBS 13:12-15

> *Hope deferred makes the heart sick, but desire fulfilled is a tree of life. The one who despises the word will be in debt to it, but the one who fears the commandment will be rewarded. The teaching of the wise is a fountain of life, to turn aside from the snares of death. Good understanding produces favor, but the way of the treacherous is hard.*

Fruit provides righteousness. We will understand and discern what God is doing and what He is refraining from doing. Consequently, our choices, decisions and actions will become much clearer. We receive His righteousness and express it to others. We grow in righteousness, as the fruit of His nature becomes imputed to us.

It is victory

REVELATION 2:7

> *He who has an ear, let him hear what the Spirit says to the churches. To him who overcomes, I will grant to eat of the tree of life, which is in the Paradise of God.*

Those who share Christ's victory over self, the world and the Evil One are "Overcomers". They will eat from the tree of life in God's Kingdom and experience its wonderful fruit. The good news is we can overcome and avoid a life of failure or mediocrity. We can live a life of victory, being transformed, set free and experiencing great success. The enemy will not be able to stand against us and thwart the will of God for our lives.

It is eternal in nature

LUKE 22:15-19

> *And He said to them, "I have earnestly desired to eat this Passover with you before I suffer; for I say to you, I shall never again eat it until it is fulfilled in the kingdom of God." And when He had taken a cup and given thanks, He said, "Take this and share it among yourselves; for I say to you, I will not drink of the fruit of the vine from now on until the kingdom of God comes." And when He had taken some bread and given thanks, He broke it and gave it to them, saying, "This is My body which is given for you; do this in remembrance of Me."*

JOHN 6:48-58

> *I am the bread of life. Your fathers ate the manna in the wilderness, and they died. This is the bread which comes down out of heaven, so that one may eat of it and not die. I am the living bread that came down out of heaven; if anyone eats of this bread, he will live forever; and the bread also which I will give for the life of the world is My flesh."*

> *Then the Jews began to argue with one another, saying, "How can this man give us His flesh to eat?" So Jesus said to them, "Truly, truly, I say to you, unless you eat the flesh of the Son of Man and drink His blood, you have no life in yourselves. He who eats My flesh and drinks My blood has eternal life, and I will raise him up on the last day. For My flesh is true food, and My blood is true drink. He who eats My flesh and drinks My blood abides in Me, and I in him. As the living Father sent Me, and I live because of the Father, so he who eats Me, he also will live because of Me. This is the bread which came down out of heaven; not as the fathers ate and died; he who eats this bread will live forever."*

Fruit actually represents God and His Kingdom. He is the source of this fruit, and we are to be nourished by Him. He is the sustainer of life. We "feed" on Him by receiving and digesting His Word and by receiving the Spirit, resident within us. It emanates from the Kingdom through Christ to us. Simply because He left the Earth did not stop His production of fruit in our lives. In reality, it allowed more fruit to be borne. The ultimate benefit is our experience of eternity, now evidenced in a new way since Christ in now in charge of the Kingdom.

AN AVOCADO AVALANCHE

It was wintertime. Denny Weinberg, his wife Ally, my wife Linda and I were vacationing together at the Weinberg vacation home in Lanai, Hawaii (a spectacular place overlooking the ocean). One afternoon we were sitting together on their patio spending time in the Word as a sort of mini-retreat, just the four of us. Denny received a phone call that there was going to be a rare hard freeze in Southern California, where they live and own an avocado orchard. Even a marginal freeze will destroy the avocado crop, and if temperatures are low enough (below 28 degrees) the trees themselves could be destroyed. There is no good way to prevent of the destruction or mitigate the impact. As the four of us went to prayer, we listened to God's promises, and He spoke that He would preserve the orchard, even though the area was going to experience this freezing. He asked us to pray in faith and in unity believe His promise would be fulfilled. We did, and He did! The Weinberg orchard was fully preserved, suffered no loss, and experienced a full crop. Most other orchards within a 30-mile radius experienced significant frost damage and loss of their crops. In fact, when the Weinbergs returned home a week later, the entire county was visibly scarred with whole farms of dead trees. In the midst of them was an oasis of healthy green trees on the Weinberg farm. It was truly a miracle as God had promised, and it was visible for all to see and wonder.

A few years later, it was the normal time to harvest the crop. However, the avocados seemed rather puny and not as numerous as usual. The workers pull avocados from trees and place them in one-ton bins to deliver to the wholesaler. They asked Denny if they should even bother since there would not be much of a crop and the cost of picking would be so prohibitive. Denny asked God what to do, and He said to complete the harvest. A couple hours later, the workers were excited and asked to see Denny. When he arrived at the collection point, the pickers reported that as they were picking and placing avocados in the bins, the trees seemed to have more and more fruit on them and the sizes were somehow so much more in the bins than they appeared on the trees. Could they be multiplying in number and size as they picked? Sure enough, they needed to deliver twice the number of bins they had calculated and initially ordered. They and the Weinbergs were in awe. They experienced firsthand the miracle of the feeding of the five thousand Christ performed in Galilee. Another supernatural work of God!

A year later, early in the season, Denny and Ally's trees were blooming with many flowers, and the abundance of bees indicated a great harvest was in process. One night Denny was awakened from a deep sleep worrying the orchard crop would be so bountiful, the young trees might be damaged trying to support the fruit. Also, he worried in the rare instance all trees bore fruit that same year, there would be a risk all the trees would produce no fruit the next year. Allyson woke, aware that Denny was once again worrying about something that God had already declared. She asked, "Isn't this our sixth harvest year?" Denny could not remember, and troubled by the implication, went to the office in the middle of the night and pulled the records.

Sure enough, they were experiencing the growth of their sixth harvest year. The Father led him to Old Testament truth that promised the crop would receive a double portion in the sixth year and the seventh year was to be left fallow. They were to harvest a minimal crop for family and give the rest to the poor. Denny and Ally were truly amazed when they received two separate harvests in that sixth year (unlike nearby orchards). Further, they were obedient to the instruction to leave the seventh year fallow and sure enough, there was only minimal crop for their family and they gave the rest to the poor. Then, in the eighth year, the trend of increasing production continued and the magnitude far exceeded that of the sixth year. In fact, when production was charted, it was clear the overall trend was consistent, only the seventh year crop was folded into the sixth, allowing the trees to celebrate their Sabbath. This was accomplished completely by the hand of the master, with no input from Denny and Allyson. This experience of supernatural work, in a real orchard, verified for Denny and Ally the miraculous life of the Kingdom. They have given witness to many church audiences of the physical evidence of these supernatural works. God's heart is for us to expect this as part of a normal Kingdom life!

THOUGHTS FOR CONSIDERATION

Have you ever sorted through and examined the "fruit" in your life, both its quality and quantity? Even though we are "results-oriented" people, our tendency is to evaluate the product of our earthly activities, rather than the Father's work through us. We often assume a connection between the two when, in fact, one is a by-product of our will and pursuits and the other occurs solely through aligning ourselves with the Father, allowing Him to produce His "fruit" in our lives.

What changes do we need to make in order to allow this to happen? Do we need to re-adjust the way we plan and set goals in our lives? How do we know whose fruit is a product of our efforts? In the space provided, document your thoughts on what needs to be done in your life to ensure fruit from the "tree of life" is being produced.

_____

_____

_____

_____

_____

_____

_____

_____

CHAPTER 8

The Consequences
of Not Living a Restored Life

In Deuteronomy 30:11-20, it is revealed that God sets before us a choice of life and blessing versus death and curses. Believers will not automatically experience the life and blessings of the Kingdom. Rather, it is our choice to either live a carnal life (in the self outside the Kingdom of God) or walk in the Spirit, surrendering our will to the Father's and enjoying the blessings of the restored life. Remember, our default is to choose self, thus our decision is never neutral. If we fail to choose to walk in the Spirit, we automatically are choosing to walk in self, world and the flesh. There are serious consequences to not living a restored life.

WE MISS THE PROMISED BLESSINGS.

We will not be in a position to receive God's promised blessings but will experience difficulty, frustration and oppression in the world, which is under Satan's domain (his desire is to kill, steal and destroy). Not only do we miss the blessings but we remain subject to destruction that is consistently in the world.

Life will be difficult

LEVITICUS 26:14-21

> *But if you do not obey Me and do not carry out all these commandments, if,*
> *instead, you reject My statutes, and if your soul abhors My ordinances so as*
> *not to carry out all My commandments, and so break My covenant, I, in turn,*
> *will do this to you: I will appoint over you a sudden terror, consumption and*
> *fever that will waste away the eyes and cause the soul to pine away; also, you*
> *will sow your seed uselessly, for your enemies will eat it up. I will set My face*
> *against you so that you will be struck down before your enemies; and those who*
> *hate you will rule over you, and you will flee when no one is pursuing you.*
> *If also after these things you do not obey Me, then I will punish you seven*
> *times more for your sins. I will also break down your pride of power; I will*
> *also make your sky like iron and your earth like bronze. Your strength will be*
> *spent uselessly, for your land will not yield its produce and the trees of the land*
> *will not yield their fruit. If then, you act with hostility against Me and are*
> *unwilling to obey Me, I will increase the plague on you seven times according*
> *to your sins.*

If we refuse to remain in the Kingdom of God, to respond and be obedient to His instructions and thus break the Covenant, we will live a difficult and oppressed life. We will not only experience the enemy trying to ruin and frustrate our lives, but also God withholding His favor and allowing us to be in unpleasant places and circumstances. He desires us to respond to a simple question: "How is that (refusing the Kingdom) working for you?" Since it will not work well, He wants us to turn around, return to Him and immediately begin walking in his Kingdom. This causes the curses to cease and reestablishes the flow of Covenant blessings.

We experience the results of the Fall

DEUTERONOMY 28:15-20

> *But it shall come about, if you do not obey the LORD your God, to observe to do all His commandments and His statutes with which I charge you today, that all these curses will come upon you and overtake you: Cursed shall you be in the city, and cursed shall you be in the country. Cursed shall be your basket and your kneading bowl. Cursed shall be the offspring of your body and the produce of your ground, the increase of your herd and the young of your flock. Cursed shall you be when you come in, and cursed shall you be when you go out. The LORD will send upon you curses, confusion, and rebuke, in all you undertake to do, until you are destroyed and until you perish quickly, on account of the evil of your deeds, because you have forsaken Me.*

When we refuse to hear and follow God in His Kingdom, we actually invite the curses (evil, frustration, difficulty, pain and oppression) to be victorious. Deuteronomy 28 actually contains fifty-three verses identifying these curses. The blessings are listed in only eleven verses. However, they are so encompassing they cover all aspects of our lives. These passages are very specific because the world is so full of destruction. We need to understand the choice we make is critical, and the consequences of not choosing to walk in the Kingdom are serious.

WE WILL DEPEND ON THE WORLD'S SYSTEMS AND LEADERS TO SATISFY OUR NEEDS

While we may achieve a certain level of success in our personal goals, we will miss the fullness of all God desires as we live in His Kingdom. We certainly will miss the supernatural work of God and the fulfillment of His promises. Essentially, we will limit the joy and the beauty of all that life could be under the rule of God. Since our goals are so limited, we may achieve success in one area, but we will usually experience failure in others, such as marriage, family, ministry, character, etc. We instead look solely to the world's economic, political and governmental systems to determine our behavior and provide our needs. Our lives become reactive to these forces, never attaining a continuity and direction allowing us to move forward with certainty and confidence. What are some of the consequences of looking to the world for our answers?

We become "worldly beings" with "warped" values

ROMANS 1:20-25

For since the creation of the world His invisible attributes, His eternal power and divine nature have been clearly seen, being understood through what has been made, so that they are without excuse. For even though they knew God, they did not honor Him as God or give thanks, but they became futile in their speculations, and their foolish heart was darkened. Professing to be wise, they became fools, and exchanged the glory of the incorruptible God for an image in the form of corruptible man and of birds and four-footed animals and crawling creatures. Therefore God gave them over in the lusts of their hearts to impurity, so that their bodies would be dishonored among them. For they exchanged the truth of God for a lie and worshiped and served the creature rather than the Creator, who is blessed forever. Amen.

As we rely on the world for our satisfaction and purpose, we believe ourselves to be wise, though we are actually foolish. We exchange God's wisdom and truth for a worldly perspective. God then allows us to pursue our selfish desires. We miss the presence of God and His directing our steps into Covenant blessings. Absent is His promises and the fullness of life He has provided.

We become "foolish" in our own wisdom.

1 CORINTHIANS 1:25-29; 3:18-21

> Because the foolishness of God is wiser than men, and the weakness of God is stronger than men. For consider your calling, brethren, that there were not many wise according to the flesh, not many mighty, not many noble; but God has chosen the foolish things of the world to shame the wise, and God has chosen the weak things of the world to shame the things which are strong, and the base things of the world and the despised God has chosen, the things that are not, so that He may nullify the things that are, so that no man may boast before God...
>
> ...Let no man deceive himself. If any man among you thinks that he is wise in this age, he must become foolish, so that he may become wise. For the wisdom of this world is foolishness before God. For it is written, "He is the one who catches the wise in their craftiness"; and again, "The LORD knows the reasonings of the wise, that they are useless." So then let no one boast in men. For all things belong to you.

The wisdom of the world is actually foolishness, as it tries to nullify the beauty and wonder of God. Thus, it is really useless! Our worldly lives will then also be useless, not expressing God's purposes, but rather experiencing this foolishness and the destruction worldliness brings.

Our "results" have no value and erode

GALATIANS 6:7-8

> Do not be deceived. God is not mocked; for whatever a man sows, this he will also reap. For the one who sows to his own flesh will from the flesh reap corruption, but the one who sows to the Spirit will from the Spirit reap eternal life.

We must be discerning and understand God knows what He is doing and is not intimidated or changed by our arrogant behavior. If we are catering to our flesh (walking in our own will and serving our own selfish desires), we actually will be planting the seeds of destruction and decay. What we think will lead us to a safe and positive place will actually result in failure. Our success in seeking particular goals may seem to be beneficial, but will not be long-lasting if sown in the flesh, outside the Kingdom of God.

We become "hostile" to God

JAMES 4:2-5

> You do not have because you do not ask. You ask and do not receive, because you ask with wrong motives, so that you may spend it on your pleasures. You adulteresses, do you not know that friendship with the world is hostility toward God? Therefore whoever wishes to be a friend of the world makes himself an enemy of God. Or do you think that the Scripture speaks to no purpose: "He jealously desires the Spirit which He has made to dwell in us"?

We must fully grasp that placing our trust in the world (relying on the world as we seek our own will) is actually in opposition to God. We are really working against His purposes. If our selfish prayers are not answered, we tend to believe God is our enemy. We subsequently believe the lie that God does not really wish to bless us. This cements our desire to pursue our own selfish goals, thinking they are the only way to success, perpetuating a vicious cycle that keeps us out of the Kingdom. The remedy is to return to God, walking in His Kingdom and experiencing the promised blessings.

OUR LIVES LACK PEACE

Even if we might experience moments of happiness and peace when circumstances are favorable, we will not experience the long-lasting peace that only comes from God as we walk in the Kingdom. We need to understand the results of not experiencing His peace.

Kingdom peace differs from worldly peace

JOHN 14:27

Peace I leave with you; My peace I give to you; not as the world gives do I give to you. Do not let your heart be troubled, nor let it be fearful.

The peace of God greatly differs from a worldly sense of peace. The peace of God is not dependent on circumstances but on a relationship as we walk in the Kingdom of God. The world's peace is completely dependent on circumstances, and therefore is fleeting. Furthermore, what we might consider to be positive, peaceful circumstances could actually be opposed to God. Ultimately it could bring fear, anxiety, worry, heartache or failure.

If we only have worldly peace, our plans are frustrated and we are defeated

JEREMIAH 6:13-19

"For from the least of them even to the greatest of them, everyone is greedy for gain, and from the prophet even to the priest, everyone deals falsely. They have healed the brokenness of My people superficially, saying, 'Peace, peace,' but there is no peace. Were they ashamed because of the abomination they have done? They were not even ashamed at all; they did not even know how to blush. Therefore they shall fall among those who fall; at the time that I punish them, they shall be cast down," says the LORD. Thus says the LORD, "Stand by the ways and see and ask for the ancient paths, where the good way is, and walk in it; and you will find rest for your souls." But they said, "We will not walk in it." And I set watchmen over you, saying, "Listen to the sound of the trumpet!" But they said, "We will not listen." Therefore hear, O nations, and know, O congregation, what is among them. Hear, O earth: behold, I am

119

bringing disaster on this people, the fruit of their plans, because they have not listened to My words, and as for My law, they have rejected it also.

Worldly peace is based upon false promises and pretenses. It is a nifty trick of the enemy appearing to be positive. In fact, it does not bring peace. If we refuse to walk with God, instead seeking our own peace, our plans bring frustration and we experience anger and hostility. We also experience disappointment, pain and difficulty.

God opposes us

EZEKIEL 13:8-11

Therefore, thus says the Lord GOD, "Because you have spoken falsehood and seen a lie, therefore behold, I am against you," declares the Lord GOD. "So My hand will be against the prophets who see false visions and utter lying divinations. They will have no place in the council of My people, nor will they be written down in the register of the house of Israel, nor will they enter the land of Israel, that you may know that I am the Lord GOD. It is definitely because they have misled My people by saying, 'Peace!' when there is no peace. And when anyone builds a wall, behold, they plaster it over with whitewash; so tell those who plaster it over with whitewash, that it will fall. A flooding rain will come, and you, O hailstones, will fall; and a violent wind will break out."

The world's peace is based on falsehoods and lies, telling us the world can satisfy our needs and desires. What we think is contributing to achieving our goals, is actually working against us, bringing about destruction in our lives. What we experience will actually be of no value, and will ultimately collapse and dwindle. It lacks a solid foundation and will not stand against the purposes of God.

WE MISS GOD'S ETERNAL PLAN FOR US IN THIS LIFETIME

As we live in self, in the world, by definition we cannot join God in His eternal purposes and plans. While we may enjoy some temporal success (as defined by the world), we certainly will not be participating in expanding the Kingdom of God in and around our lives.

We follow forces opposed to God

MATTHEW 16:21-23

> *From that time Jesus began to show His disciples that He must go to Jerusalem, and suffer many things from the elders and chief priests and scribes, and be killed, and be raised up on the third day. Peter took Him aside and began to rebuke Him, saying, "God forbid it, Lord! This shall never happen to You." But He turned and said to Peter, "Get behind Me, Satan! You are a stumbling block to Me; for you are not setting your mind on God's interests, but man's."*

God's eternal purposes included sending His own Son to die on a cross and be resurrected into eternal life. If we are not aligned with Him, we actually act on behalf of Satan (the Evil One). We are to conform to the mind of Christ, rather than living our own selfish interest.

We experience judgment and expose ourselves to death

JOHN 5:20-24

> *For the Father loves the Son, and shows Him all things that He Himself is doing; and the Father will show Him greater works than these, so that you will marvel. For just as the Father raises the dead and gives them life, even so the Son also gives life to whom He wishes. For not even the Father judges anyone, but He has given all judgment to the Son, so that all will honor the Son even as they honor the Father. He who does not honor the Son does not honor the Father who sent Him. Truly, truly, I say to you, he who hears My word, and*

believes Him who sent Me, has eternal life, and does not come into judgment,
but has passed out of death into life.

God's eternal purposes are for His supernatural works to be manifest in our lives, demonstrating His very existence, power and truth. As people witness this, they too will be drawn from worldy destruction into life eternal.

We miss our eternal experience here on Earth

2 TIMOTHY 1:5-12

For I am mindful of the sincere faith within you, which first dwelt in your grandmother Lois and your mother Eunice, and I am sure that it is in you as well. For this reason I remind you to kindle afresh the gift of God which is in you through the laying on of my hands. For God has not given us a spirit of timidity, but of power and love and discipline. Therefore do not be ashamed of the testimony of our Lord or of me His prisoner, but join with me in suffering for the gospel according to the power of God, who has saved us and called us with a holy calling, not according to our works, but according to His own purpose and grace which was granted us in Christ Jesus from all eternity, but now has been revealed by the appearing of our Savior Christ Jesus, who abolished death and brought life and immortality to light through the gospel, for which I was appointed a preacher and an apostle and a teacher. For this reason I also suffer these things, but I am not ashamed; for I know whom I have believed and I am convinced that He is able to guard what I have entrusted to Him until that day.

God's eternal purpose is to provide grace to all people through Christ. Jesus abolished death and through His resurrection provided access to abundant life and immortality (everlasting life with Him). If we are ashamed of representing Him (which will be true if we're walking in the flesh, in the world), we will not experience real and abundant life, nor offer it to others. We will miss being a part of God's bigger story of expanding the Kingdom, inviting others to be excited about the Gospel and speaking it freely and openly.

SUMMARY

I think there is a void in every heart from the time of birth until the moment of spiritual rebirth. As we have seen, this void can continue even after we accept the gift of Christ. What is missing is the fullness of life only the Father can provide. We seek to fill that void through earthly means, but are never satisfied. Still, we continue to try. In many cases, worldly efforts are the only means we know. We have not been taught otherwise. In other cases, we remain more comfortable with worldly and self-induced methods, even though they have consistently failed to produce the desired results. Any benefits received are very short-term.

The void continues and we recognize there must be more to this life on Earth than we are currently receiving. Tullian Tchividjian describes the "nagging sense that there had to be more to life than what I was experiencing—there had to be more to who I was than what this world was telling me." (Tullian Tchvidijan, *One Way Love*). This is the void and consequences described in this section. We really miss our life experience, settling for a far inferior, worldly one. Instead of truly living, we have reduced our lives to mere existing. The difference is immense.

LET'S MOVE FORWARD

As we contemplate the condition of our lives, the beauty of the life available through Christ and the darkness of life without Him, we recognize the need of a "call to action" on our part. Why would we desire to miss the mark or pay the price of a misdirected and unfulfilled life? Why waste this precious, unique time when we are able to both exist on the earth *and* dwell in the Kingdom of God? Let's all begin to take the steps necessary to reduce or eliminate the possibility of that happening. As we contemplate the need to move to a restored life, what are three or four necessary and immediate actions that need to undertaken?

_____

_____

_____

_____

_____

_____

_____

_____

_____

_____

_____

_____

_____

CHAPTER 9

Conclusion

Now that this book is completed, we should feel differently about life than when we began. We need to reassess our answers to the questions in Chapter 1 (The Big Picture). We should recognize a unique paradigm in our lives as a result of the reality of the Kingdom of God.

The Bible clearly points to a different life available for believers in Christ. Will we now move to take hold of that life and its promises and blessings? Or will we stay on our own path, content with our own agendas, efforts and the rewards they have provided? Will we remain satisfied with a "less than abundant" life? That's the challenge that lies before us. Here are some suggestions to move into the awesome experience the Father has prepared.

ENJOY THE PRESENCE OF THE FATHER

We really enjoy being with our spouses. It's a blessing to see them first thing in the morning and to say "good night". We try to plan things together and to spend as much time together as possible.

We also enjoy our family of children and grandchildren. It's always a great time just to "hang together" as well as go on vacations and celebrate holidays and special times with them. Their presence fills us with joy and thankfulness.

We also like to be with friends. Time with special people in our lives is such a joy. Each time the Cases' and Colletts' get together is a blast.

There are others in our lives whose fellowship is cherished and we jump at the opportunity to be with them

How do we feel about being with the Father? Do we have this level of joy and anticipation? Do we join Him with excitement and expectation? Do we feel "at home" and at peace when we are with Him? If not, why? It's probably because we haven't spent enough consistent time with Him or cultivated His presence and relationship to the point where we begin to really know and enjoy Him. In order for this to happen, we must move from a ritual of prayer to a relationship of communication with Him. As this happens, we will enter a relationship that surpasses any other life experience.

GET IT SETTLED!

One of Rich's favorite exhortations is to "Get it Settled." In making this statement, he refers to our need to accept what Scripture says as truth and reality. Once we take this step, we can move to a higher level of experiential reality in our lives. Until we do so, scripture remains in our minds as theological understanding or religious knowledge. It will not be manifest or witnessed in our daily living.

There are several things we need to get settled. The first is we were created to experience God and to let Him govern our lives. His objective is to pour an anointing of blessings on us. Secondly, we need to accept the reality of the Kingdom of God. There is, indeed, another realm beyond the planet and universe in which we currently reside. Unlike our world, it is eternal in nature and works much differently than earthly systems and governments. We should connect our lives to the Kingdom and join His bigger story, allowing Him to impact our lives and the lives of others.

Thirdly, we need to understand the completeness of the work of Christ. He changed the results of the Fall. Through Jesus, the Father has again made His Kingdom and resources available. This is not theory, but reality. We must begin to constantly seek the Father for everything and begin to experience His supernatural love and power in all our relationships and activities. Finally, we need to grasp the newness of life we have been given in Christ and accept the fact the Trinity resides within us. We have all the connectivity we need to pursue life vigorously and abundantly. There is no limit to what can be done through Christ. Through Him, we are able to think, act and bear fruit at a level previously unknown and unseen. This newness is our eternity becoming a present reality.

So, let's get it settled! Let's move on to this marvelous life provided by a God "who is able to do far more than we can ever think or imagine."

MAKE A CHOICE

In the great chapter of Deuteronomy 30, Moses sets a choice before the nation of Israel. He states he has set before them "life and death, blessings and curse." He asks them to "choose life so they and their offspring may live." Near the end of his life, Joshua gives a similar charge to the nation (Joshua 24:15). He asks them to "choose this day whom you will serve," adding "as for me and my house, we will serve the Lord."

We tend to think both men were talking about a one-time choice. In response to Joshua, the people clearly stated they would "serve the Lord, for He is our God" (verse 18). In reality, this identifies a choice to be made on a daily basis. Once we "get it settled," we then make a daily decision to allow those realities to infiltrate our lives. Each day provides the opportunity to "opt out" of God's divine plan and revelation. He allows us to make that choice. If we make no choice or choose to go it alone, the bottom line is we miss the blessings and experience of the fullness of life. All the settled truth we previously encountered becomes "unsettled" again. We revert back to our earthly existence, separate from the Father and ignorant of the impact of Christ on our lives and the world.

Fortunately, there is another way. Each day we can wake up and say, "Yes, Lord, yes! I commit this day to you, through Christ. I desire to dwell in Your Kingdom, driven and guided by your Spirit of truth and holiness. I choose to be your child and experience the life you created me to have. Let's get going!" Intentionally making that daily decision gives us immediate focus and direction, putting opposing forces on notice.

Choose you this day! Choose life! Choose the Father and His Kingdom!

About the Authors

Larry Collett was an employee of Cass Information Systems from 1963 until his retirement in July 2008. He is currently the Chairman of the Board. He was hired by the company's banking subsidiary, Cass Commercial Bank, and held numerous positions culminating in his appointment as Executive Vice President in 1974. In 1990, he was elected Chief Executive Officer of Cass Information Systems, Inc. and was given the additional responsibilities of Board Chairman in 1992.

In 2007, Mr. Collett was named one of the nations best CEOs by DeMarche Associates, Inc., a Kansas City-based consulting company. Cass was also named by *Forbes* magazine as one of the nation's top 200 small public companies in 2006 and 2008. Cass is also a member of the Russell 2000, a well-recognized list of public companies selected for inclusion in this highly respected investment fund.

Larry's leadership combines two aspects of his life: a passion for new technology and a deeply held faith. His drive to incorporate newer technologies and his insistence on trusting God have been key ingredients of his business career.

In addition to his business responsibilities, Mr. Collett has held numerous positions with civic, charitable and church-related institutions. He was the Chairman of the Greater St. Louis Billy Graham Crusade in 1999. He also worked with several organizations that bring churches and pastors together in the St. Louis region. Larry chaired numerous fundraising activities for non-profit and educational institutions. He is a member of the Board of Regents of Trinity International University and Seminary in Deerfield, Illinois.

He has been a teacher of several courses for business, church and non-profit institutions. He is a member of the CEO Forum, an organization of Christian CEOs, and is on the adjunct teaching staff for the Spiritual Leadership Institute (SLI) of that organization. He has authored several

Bible studies, primarily related to the topics of "Abiding in Christ" and "Kingdom Restoration."

He attended St. Louis University, where he obtained both undergraduate and graduate degrees. He also performed post-graduate work at Rutgers University through the Stonier School of Banking. In 2014 he received the "Outstanding Alumni Award" from St. Louis University's Graduate School of Business.

A lifelong resident of the St. Louis area, Mr. Collett has been married to his wife Sharon since 1965. They have three children and nine grandchildren.

Richard T. Case, age 65, has over 45 years of executive line management experience, both as a senior executive with Fortune 500 companies and as a management consultant to numerous industries and companies. He has also been a featured speaker at numerous conferences and seminars. Mr. Case has received *The Wall Street Journal* Achievement Award, and is listed in *Who's Who in American Business*. Mr. Case holds an MBA degree from the University of Southern California where he graduated with a 4.0 GPA, first in the class; and a BS degree in Management and Finance from Bradley University, *magna cum laude*. He also graduated with a seminary Masters degree from Trinity Evangelical Divinity School, *summa cum laude*.

He and his wife, Linda, have started several new churches that remain strong today, and have served as interim pastors of troubled churches, bringing reconciliation and new vision to these situations. Currently, he and Linda are leading a fruitful, Christian marriage retreat ministry, "All for Jesus Living Waters Retreat Ministry". In addition to the retreats they personally lead, they now have over 16 couples trained as leaders who are conducting marriage retreats in their respective geographies around the country. Mr. Case is a published author, has hosted a weekly business radio program, and has served as a strategic consultant to numerous non-profit organizations, including CEO Forum, Focus on the Family, and Navigators.

Richard lives in Castle Rock, Colorado, with his wife of 45 years. They both enjoy their five grandchildren and three grown children.

Authors' Note

Richard and Larry were given an assignment by the Father many years ago to receive understanding and revelation from the Word and communion with the Spirit about the Kingdom of God and the beauty of a "restored life." They then collaborated on this book (and a second volume) to offer fellow believers what they have received. Understanding the Kingdom of God is critical to a believer's fulfillment of God's intended life for us. Through their understanding, living out these principles and now teaching them to others, they have established a reputation for helping others to live out a restored life in the Kingdom.

Additional Notes